Copyright © 2025 by Katalin Malatinszky, Astrological Design By Katalin

All rights reserved.
No portion of this book may be reproduced in any way without written permission from the author.
This non-fiction book is intended to introduce the connection between Astrology and Interior Design. It is written for entertainment purposes only. This avant-garde approach inspires your creative side and teaches you more about your divine self, helping you toward a more balanced life. The content of this book is not intended to supplement the care provided by a qualified professional.

The book is sold with the understanding that neither the author nor the publisher is responsible, makes no representations or warranties concerning the completeness of the book's contents, and expressly disclaims any implied warranties of merchantability or fitness for a particular purpose. The author or publisher assumes no responsibility for errors or omissions in the content of this book.

Consider hiring a professional when needed, as the advice and strategies herein may not suit your situation. Neither the author nor the publisher shall be liable for any loss of profit or other commercial damages, including but not limited to special, incidental, consequential, personal, or other damages.

Book Cover by Katalin Malatinszky and a technical collaborator
or technicality
Illustrations by Katalin Malatinszky and a technical collaborator
Royalty-free images by Canva
Edition 02 - 2025
ISBN: 978-1-0689398-0-8
www.astrologicaldesign.com
Publisher: Katalin Malatinszky
copyright

ASTROLOGICAL INTERIOR DESIGN

ASTROLOGY ~ INTERIOR DESIGN - CONSCIOUS LIFESTYLE

Discover the Hidden World of Astrological Design

Katalin Malatinszky

Interior Decorator & Astrology Enthusiast

Astrological Design Consultant

TABLE OF CONTENTS

GRATITUDE - 7
A couple of words to reflect my gratitude

DEDICATION - 9
I wrote this book in dedication to my two girls.

INSIGHTS - 11
A quick insight into what the book is about

WELCOME - 13
A short note about the intention of the book

MY STORY - 17
A little about the author

INTRODUCTION ASTROLOGY & DESIGN - 23
Introduction to Astrology

INTRODUCTION ASTROLOGY & DESIGN - 33
Introduction to Interior Design

CHAPTER 1: ARIES - 38
Aries Astrological traits ~ Interior Design Style ~ Feng Shui

CHAPTER 2: TAURUS - 50
Taurus Astrological traits ~ Interior Design Style ~ Feng Shui

CHAPTER 3: GEMINI - 62
Gemini Astrological traits ~ Interior Design Style ~ Feng Shui

TABLE OF CONTENTS

CHAPTER 4: CANCER - 74

Cancer Astrological traits ~ Interior Design Style ~ Feng Shui

CHAPTER 5: LEO - 86

Leo Astrological traits ~ Interior Design Style ~ Feng Shui

CHAPTER 6: VIRGO - 98

Virgo Astrological traits ~ Interior Design Style ~ Feng Shui

CHAPTER 7: LIBRA - 110

Libra Astrological traits ~ Interior Design Style ~ Feng Shui

CHAPTER 8: SCORPIO - 122

Scorpio Astrological traits ~ Interior Design Style ~ Feng Shui

CHAPTER 9: SAGITTARIUS - 134

Sagittarius Astrological traits ~ Interior Design Style ~ Feng Shui

CHAPTER 10: CAPRICORN - 146

Capricorn Astrological traits ~ Interior Design Style ~ Feng Shui

CHAPTER 11: AQUARIUS - 158

Aquarius Astrological traits ~ Interior Design Style ~ Feng Shui

CHAPTER 12: PISCES - 170

Pisces Astrological traits ~ Interior Design Style ~ Feng Shui

REWARD - 183

Fruition ~ Success ~ Fulfillments

ASTROLOGY
INTERIOR DESIGN
CONSCIOUS LIFESTYLE

DISCOVER THE HIDDEN WORLD
OF ASTROLOGICAL DESIGN

GRATITUDE

I am humbly grateful for the incredible life journey
With all the blessings and challenges
That led me to write this book.

~

Dear Sophia, your talent behind the lens and ability to capture the moment's emotions and essence are remarkable. Thank you for your professionalism and for making me comfortable in front of the camera. I am incredibly grateful for your patience when taking pictures of my doggies. Your passion for your craft shines throughout the photoshoots, and memories are beautifully preserved.

~

Sweet Tatyana, your talent in graphic design has been a significant staple for my vision for the aesthetics of my book to come alive.
Your detail-oriented personality and explicit graphic design knowledge have made my manuscript a work of art and brought my vision alive. Working with you has been an absolute pleasure, and I am incredibly grateful for your expertise and willingness to go the extra mile.

~

Thank you from the bottom of my heart for your exceptional work. I am excited to share my book with the world, and your talent will continue to captivate readers for years.

Much Love,

Katalin

ASTROLOGY
INTERIOR DESIGN
CONSCIOUS LIFESTYLE

DISCOVER THE HIDDEN WORLD
OF ASTROLOGICAL DESIGN

DEDICATION

My deepest gratitude goes to my two exceptional girls,

Stephanie and Angelika,

I cannot begin to tell you how much you both mean to me.

Life has had its ups and downs, but you are both pushing through.

Nothing ever was handed to you, and that made you who you are today.

Your strength, hard work, courage and determination are so inspiring.

I am so impressed that you both follow your hearts and dreams,

rescue animals and are proud of your heritage.

The Love of underprivileged animals speaks so highly of your character and integrity.

I couldn't be prouder, Mami, that you chose to save and rescue dogs and bunnies.

Even when your life circumstances were challenging, moving from one country to

another and selflessly putting the bunnies and doggies first, never leave them behind.

I know you both will make a difference in the world. And I couldn't be happier.

Although you are still young, I am thrilled and proud of who you are

You both became kind and wonderful human beings.

Our journeys are intertwined with many karmic cycles and experiences.

You have taught me so much that I am so grateful for.

May all your dreams and wishes come true.

My most tremendous gratitude in life is to you,

Stephanie & Angelika

I love you more than words can say,

If money were no object,
What would your home look like?

Your most intimate space is an extension of you, and
When consciously designing your chic essence and flair,
Your sanctuary will align with your unique nature and charm.

Discover The Hidden World of Astrological Design

INSIGHTS

Designing a living space that resonates with your personality and promoting personal growth can be challenging yet rewarding. Your true, authentic self and unique traits and flair can change the feel of your environment through colours, furniture, layout, or personal touches.

Blending your Astrological blueprint into your interior decor and fashion style is an innovative, unquestionably avant-garde and head-of-its-time approach that adds a personal touch to your fashion style and space.

Your horoscope can influence your preferences for colours, materials, and decorative elements, directly affecting your conscious and subconscious mind. It can support your daily routines and activities, creating functional areas that align with your personality, work, and self-care and contribute to your overall well-being.

Your personal development is a continual, ongoing journey. You must occasionally reflect on yourself, including your family dynamics, and reevaluate and rearrange your intimate, sacred space as you evolve, flourish, and thrive.

ASTROLOGY
INTERIOR DESIGN
CONSCIOUS LIFESTYLE

DISCOVER THE HIDDEN WORLD
OF ASTROLOGICAL DESIGN

WELCOME

Interior design and astrology are often found in different sentences; however, their ideologies share the same center stage in my book.

Both fields have a deep-seated, profound natural wisdom with many layers and approaches.

My passion for Design and Astrology goes back to my teen years. I have been curious about the ancient world and self-studied the connection and similarities between these two distinct yet complementary worlds.

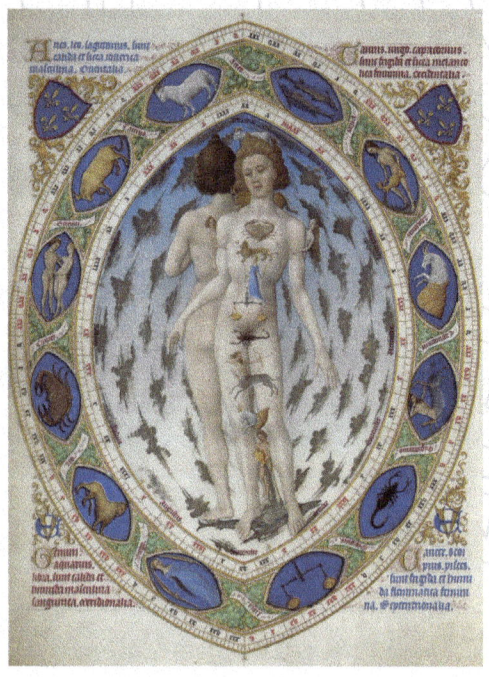

This book sheds light on your astrological traits, suggesting colours, furniture, and design styles that energetically align with the natural elements, unique personality, and characteristics you were born with.

The book provides guidance, helps you learn and capitalize on your natural gifts, and explains how to enhance your environment to support your physical, mental, and emotional well-being.

As you transform and evolve through a natural progression of life, your home or workspace is bound to align.

Although this book does not focus on the ancient philosophy of Feng Shui, it is essential to mention that this practice, over 3000 years old, is based on astrology and the common thread of incorporating the elements of the natural world.

The book is designed for those intrigued by the profound meaning of life and have a spiritual connection to their home and environment, seeking a peculiar design style and sharing the same curiosity and passion for Astrology and Interior Design.

ASTROLOGY
INTERIOR DESIGN
CONSCIOUS LIFESTYLE

DISCOVER THE HIDDEN WORLD
OF ASTROLOGICAL DESIGN

MY STORY

Intrigued by nature and searching for answers to life, my journey led me to explore various philosophies and beliefs. I was eager to find the deeper connection between my two passions, Design and Astrology.

I have been fortunate to receive my junior education in an experimental teaching system in Budapest, Hungary, my hometown and country. This exclusionary elementary school system blended music, mathematics, and art, and I still use it today. Later, I attended a guild-style trade school, where I studied designing and handcrafting high-quality custom leather garments. My European flair for education and creativity gave me the foundation and influenced my interest in
learning interior decorating and design.
My trade and craft of custom sewing from back home allowed me to overcome the language barrier when I came to Canada, almost Thirty-six years ago, in 1988.

My passion for design and learning led me to take and complete the Interior Decorating course at Seneca College in 2003. After finishing the program, I specialized in residential custom window coverings and upholstery, blending my craft of custom sewing and newly gained interior design knowledge. I designed and hand-sewn draperies and helped my clients select furniture and finishes while raising my two girls.

I adored my work but never felt intellectually stimulated or satisfied. Self-development and self-education have been a daily routine in my life. For over two decades, my deep interest in ancient cultures and wisdom led me to explore Colour Theory, Human Psychology, Numerology, Sacred Geometry, Feng Shui, and Astrology.

I completed multiple courses, became a Certified Feng Shui Specialist in 2018, and got Certified in Professional Organizing in 2019. I have been fascinated by the beauty of nature and have always felt drawn to the natural world.

Life's journey, challenges, and tough times have significantly transformed my personal and professional life in the last several years. Exploring various philosophies, beliefs, and ancient wisdom allowed me to realize the greater connection between our inner world and personal space, including interior design principles and natural elements (Fire, Earth, Air, and Water) of astrology.

This mystical intelligence surrounds your homes, workspace and environment. Your most intimate space is an extension of you, and Your aura (your energetic field) directly reflects and affects your unique personality and flair.

Your astrological natal chart is a cosmic map reflecting each planet's position at the time of your birth. It gives you an insight into the specific dominant elements, such as fire, earth, air, and water, that you instinctively carry and sheds light on your personality traits, flair, likes, and dislikes.

My vision and philosophy blend these teachings of Interior Design and your Astrological blueprint to help capitalize on your natural gifts and enhance your physical space and emotional well-being as you create your temple.

I am thrilled to share what I have learned through my transformation and journey. I am happy to bring this exclusive and avant-garde path if you seek a more holistic approach to designing your exceptional sanctuary.

ASTROLOGY
INTERIOR DESIGN
CONSCIOUS LIFESTYLE

DISCOVER THE HIDDEN WORLD
OF ASTROLOGICAL DESIGN

A Personal Message Close to My Heart

Many homeless abandoned animals desperately seek a forever loving family and home. Animal shelters and rescue organizations are full of pets waiting to be adopted. Unfortunately, not all make it to their dream family. There is a vast misconception that rescued dogs or cats have many psychological or physical health issues. It may be true in some cases, but not all.

I am so happy that our family has rescued seven doggies combined in memory of our Angel, a Golden Retriever, who was from a breeder and passed away from aggressive lymphoma at age six. Thankfully all our rescue puppies are perfect mental and physical health. Rescuing our furry babies was the best decision we have ever made. Saving the lives of animals is a blessing.

If you are contemplating getting a pet, please consider adopting an animal from a shelter or a rescue organization.

Please be responsible; rescuing a pet becomes with a lifelong responsibility.

Please consult the future owner before considering giving an animal. Your reward is unconditional love, and you cannot put a price on it.

Much love, Katalin

ASTROLOGY
INTERIOR DESIGN
CONSCIOUS LIFESTYLE

DISCOVER THE HIDDEN WORLD
OF ASTROLOGICAL DESIGN

INTRODUCTION
ASTROLOGY & DESIGN

ASTROLOGY

Astrology and horoscopes have been widespread among people for thousands of years. Various cultures and ethnicities have wanted to know how their zodiac signs affected their health, relationships, and prosperity.

Astrology is an ancient science that studies and follows the constellations, the astronomical cycles of planets, cosmic objects, stars, and their influences on human consciousness and lives.
Astrology originated and was practiced in
The ancient world, in Mesopotamia and Babylonia
In the 3rd millennium BCE, around 5000 years ago.
Hellenistic astrology adopted and further developed the ancient philosophy during the Hellenistic period in the Mediterranean region from the 1st century BC and became the original tradition of Western astrology practiced by many astrologers today.

INTRODUCTION
ASTROLOGY

Ancient philosophers like Plato, Socrates, Pythagoras, Aristotle and Hippocrates were fascinated by this ancient wisdom of antiquity. They dedicated their lives to studying the cosmos and the knowledge of the ancient world: philosophy and the spiritual effect on human lives. These foundational philosophers explored, revolutionized, and merged old belief systems of Mesopotamia and created a system of Sacred Geometry, Numerology and Astrology.

Human civilizations, cultures and traditions have adopted and created a version of astrological calendars, systems and methods, such as the Mayan and Aztec calendars. People believed the Sun, Moon, planets, and other celestial bodies had shaped their personalities, affected their romantic relationships, and predicted their economic fortune.

INTRODUCTION
ASTROLOGY

Famous mathematicians, scientists, and astronomers like Galileo Galilei, an Italian astronomer, Leonardo da Vinci, and Isaac Newton were also infatuated with this wisdom and incorporated symbols into their art and work.

Dr. Carl Jung, the contemporary Swiss analytical psychologist from 1875 to 1961, was also intrigued by the Chinese divination text, I Ching (Book of Changes) and Astrology. He researched the connection between the human psyche, the Astrological elements, and colour psychology and incorporated this intelligence in treating patients in his practice.

There are three main types of Astrological philosophies, but not limited to. Tropical Astrology is based on the seasons and is mainly used in the Western world today. Sidereal Astrology follows fixed stars of the sky, and Vedic Astrology follows the unequal constellations of the sky.

INTRODUCTION
ASTROLOGY

Astrology divides the zodiacal belt or wheel into twelve houses, each associated with a particular area of life, like self, personal values, communications, home and family, other people's money and partnership.
Each zodiac sign represents a specific astrological house, mirroring the fundamental ingredients, signifying a distinct archetype and expressing its characteristics and traits.

In the universal law of polarities, feminine and masculine (non-gender specific) energies are alternating qualities of each zodiac sign throughout the zodiac wheel.
Fire and air signs carry masculine, active power,
Earth and water signs relay the feminine energy.
The virtue of polarity and astrology is also a staple part of the ancient philosophy of Feng Shui, the yin/yang or feminine/masculine concept, which is the universal language and balance of creation.

INTRODUCTION
ASTROLOGY

The four elements of the natural world in Astrology are Fire, Earth, Air, and Water, and each signifies a specific zodiac sign and its personality traits.

Fire Signs, like Aries, Leo, and Sagittarius, are known for their energetic charisma and enthusiasm and tend to be outgoing, dynamic, and adventurous.

Earth Signs, like Taurus, Virgo, and Capricorn, are reliable, grounded, practical, value stability and security, and can bring ideas into reality.

Air Signs, like Gemini, Libra, and Aquarius, identify with communication, intellectual and social attributes and academic pursuits and are known for their curious and scholastic mind and love of learning.

The Water signs, like Cancer, Scorpio, and Pisces, are creative, emotional, intuitive, and empathetic, deeply connected to their feelings and the feelings of others.

INTRODUCTION
ASTROLOGY

The twelve astrological houses are divisions of the celestial sphere, each associated with specific themes and aspects of life. In addition, each of the twelve zodiac signs carries the traits and characteristics of their ruling planets. For example, Aries's ruling planet is Mars, and Aries people are naturally passionate and forceful, symbolizing the warrior archetype of Mars. The placements of the planets in a specific zodiacal house reveal and give insight into the individual's tendencies, weaknesses and strengths.

In astrology, planetary aspects refer to the angular relationships between planets as seen from Earth. These aspects are believed to influence the energies and interactions between the planets, affecting various areas of life and personality traits.

These components are crucial in understanding and interpreting the complex astrological birth or natal chart.

INTRODUCTION
ASTROLOGY

ASTROLOGICAL HOUSES & ASPECTS OF LIFE

1st House (Ascendant/Rising Sign, Sun Ascending, East):

- ~ Ego, identity, self-image, appearance
- ~ How others perceive you
- ~ Beginnings, self-awareness

2nd House:

- ~ Finances, material possessions
- ~ Self-worth and values
- ~ Personal resources and possessions

3rd Third House:

- ~ Communication, learning, and thinking
- ~ Siblings, neighbours, and short trips
- ~ Early education and skills

4th House (Imum Coeli/IC " in Latin, Earth):

- ~ Home, family, Ancestry, and childhood
- ~ The inner sense of security, emotional foundation
- ~ Private and personal

INTRODUCTION
ASTROLOGY

5th House:
- ~ Creativity, self-expression, and pleasure
- ~ Romance, love affairs, and children
- ~ Artistic talents and hobbies

6th House:
- ~ Health, work, daily routines, and pets
- ~ Service, duty, and responsibility
- ~ Daily tasks and habits

7th House (Descendant/DC, Sun descending, West):
- ~ Partnerships, marriage, and relationships
- ~ Open enemies and conflicts
- ~ Projection of qualities onto others

8th House:
- ~ Shared resources, taxes, debt, loans
- ~ Transformation, the subconscious mind
- ~ Sexuality, Occultism, mysticism

9th House:
- ~ Higher education, philosophy, and beliefs
- ~ Long-distance travel and exploration
- ~ Spirituality, ethics, and cultural experiences

INTRODUCTION
ASTROLOGY

10th House (Midheaven/MC, Medium Coeli in Latin, Sky):
- ~ Success, Career, public image, and reputation
- ~ Ambitions, achievements, and goals
- ~ Parental Influences and Authorities

11th House:
- ~ Friendships, social networks, and groups
- ~ Aspirations and goals within the community
- ~ Humanitarian concerns and group activities

12th House:
- ~ Dreams, intuition, and spirituality
- ~ Karmic patterns, Self-sacrifice, isolation
- ~ Collective unconscious limitations

This basic introductory explanation of the essence of Astrology is only a drop in the vast sea of cosmic wisdom and is intended to intrigue the curious mind. The zodiac signs are more of a roadmap for personality traits and can be valuable when designing a personal space.

ASTROLOGY
INTERIOR DESIGN
CONSCIOUS LIFESTYLE

DISCOVER THE HIDDEN WORLD
OF ASTROLOGICAL DESIGN

INTRODUCTION
ASTROLOGY & INTERIOR DESIGN

INTERIOR DESIGN

In the past decade, digital technology has connected almost everything. Emerging technologies have provided comfort, yet people feel disconnected, lonely or isolated.

Many dream of a beautiful, peaceful, emotionally balanced home and surroundings. Searching for comfort and a deeper connection to the immediate environment and surroundings is one of the reasons people feel they need to redesign or redecorate their homes. Bringing fresh energy is necessary to shape balance in private and professional life. Our home or office affects us physically, psychologically and emotionally.

Interior design is the art and science of enhancing the interior, architecture, and surroundings and creating a more aesthetically pleasing and functional environment.

INTRODUCTION
INTERIOR DESIGN

Interior Design involves the thoughtful arrangement of furniture, colour schemes, textures, lighting, and decorative elements to transform a room into a harmonious environment. Incorporating design principles when designing a space is paramount, as it shapes not only the visual appeal but also the functionality and overall experience of the room. Interior Design not only focuses on the visual appeal of a space but also considers the emotional and practical aspects of life that contribute to the overall comfort, adaptability, and purpose of the area.

Blending the core principles of Design helps create a well-thought-out and balanced space. Interior Design principles, such as balance, harmony, rhythm, and proportion, guide the arrangement of elements to form a cohesive and pleasing atmosphere and become optimized for their intended purpose: a home, office, or public area.

INTRODUCTION
INTERIOR DESIGN

Careful design enhances traffic flow, maximizes natural light, and promotes efficient use of space. Moreover, it cultivates an ambiance that aligns with the desired mood, making the room more inviting. Emerging design principles transform spaces into meaningful and purposeful spaces that cater to aesthetic and practical needs, ultimately enriching the lives of those who inhabit them.

PRINCIPLES

~Space: Determining an area's furniture layout and functionality to optimize traffic flow.
~Colour: Selecting an appropriate colour palette that sets the mood, enhances the space, and complements the room's purpose.
~Scale: Ensuring that furniture and decorative elements are proportionate to the size of the space.

INTRODUCTION
INTERIOR DESIGN

~Unity & Rhythm: Creating a cohesive design that ties together, various materials and elements and maintains consistency throughout the space.

~Texture: Blending multiple textures and materials, such as fabrics, wood, metal, and stone add depth and tactile interest in the space.

-Balance & Symmetry: Visual balance is achieved by strategically placing symmetrical objects, furniture, or colours.

~Lighting Design: Planning and implementing lighting solutions that provide the proper illumination for various activities and contribute to the room's ambiance.

~Furniture: Selecting and arranging pieces that suit the space style to maximize comfort and appeal.

INTRODUCTION
INTERIOR DESIGN

~Accessories: Adding accessories, artwork, textiles, and
decorative pieces that reflect the personality
and style of the occupants while enhancing
The overall design.

~Functionality: Design focusing on practical use ensures
The space serves its intended purpose.

~Sustainability: Integrating eco-friendly and sustainable
materials, applications, and design
practices to minimize environmental
Impact and promote sustainable living.

Incorporating the homeowner's astrological natal chart can be beneficial when designing homes, offices, and commercial spaces. Understanding the client's true nature and translating it into a space creates an environment that reflects and aligns with their identity and celestial nature.

CHAPTER 1
ARIES

Aries folks have enough energy to power a small city. They are confident walking into a room as if they own the place.

They thrive on adventure, and their courageous, fearless personalities can climb mountains and dive into new experiences.
These independent superheroes, with their superpower, would fly if they could, but it would be "Flying Solo."

Aries takes the initiative and takes advantage of opportunities to knock on their door. The impulsive Aries prefers the short-term plan, and their saving grace is their positive attitude and willingness to work full force ahead.

The competitive play with a determined Aries is a high-stakes game where they'll trade their last dollar, and they will not stop. This is also true when it comes to their passion. It becomes their obsession.

The spontaneous Aries blossoms on last-minute plans. However, their short-tempered patience is fragile. Nothing is personal when it comes to Aries. They are straightforward communicators; diplomacy is not their strong suit.

Embracing Aries's hilarious quirks and traits is all part of the fun. Remember, if you're ever on an adventure with an Aries, be prepared for surprises, laughter, and energy!

CHAPTER 1
ARIES

PERSONALITY/ELEMENTS/ RULING PLANET

Each zodiac sign signifies a specific archetype representing unique characteristics aligned with the zodiacal house or section of the heavens. Aries is the zodiac's first sign, representing Astrology's first house, signifying personality, identity, self-expression, "Self/Ego," and life direction. Starting the Lunar New Year on March 20th to April 19th, it initiates spring with its most direct attributes.

As the first fire sign, Aries is known for their energetic passion and enthusiasm. They tend to be creative, assertive, dynamic, and adventurous, driven by inspiration and are often quick to take action, with a burning desire for self-expression.

The first fire sign of the zodiac embodies the fire element and the Yang/Masculine (non-gender specific) energy of impulsive passion, which comes forthright for Aries people. The exceedingly dynamic Yang attributes are hugely active and physical, with initiative and leadership qualities.

Aries illustrates the first house of the astrological wheel, a toddler or young child's spontaneous, sometimes chaotic human quality, all about the Self and physical body, which explains why Aries people are inclined to communicate impulsively and, more often than not, throw a temper tantrum. When feeling unheard or confronted.

CHAPTER 1
ARIES

The ruling planet of the zodiac sign, Aries, is the impulsive and fiery Mars. It's also known as The Planet of Wars. Aries people are generally truth seekers, ready to fight for their truth or beliefs and carry courageous and heroic qualities. They must release their impatient and frustrated energies and stay physically, mentally, and sexually active to avoid impulsive aggression or boredom.

As a Cardinal fire sign, Aries carries an initiator quality, is highly creative and is a fantastic person to launch a project quickly. They are excellent at developing new ideas and starting new projects.

Aries people may need help from others to stay focused and loyal to complete a long-term job or plan as they continually seek adventure, the next best thing in life.

Aries are known for their leadership qualities, independence, and pioneering spirit. Aries individuals are often bold, competitive, and enthusiastic about new challenges. Ample sleep is necessary to lower the temperature of the quick, fiery Aries to avoid bursting out at others and boost the focus and the patience of people around.

CHAPTER 1
ARIES

Aries are fast, impulsive, and reasonably generous, which explains why they quickly spend money. Like falling in love with humans, they quickly fall in love with items and worldly things. They tend to make fast financial decisions in the blink of an eye without thinking, creating short-lived amusements that are or can be costly.

This exceptionally social Fire sign enjoys meeting new people and feels comfortable in large gatherings and busy environments. They love being the life of the party and thrive on meeting new people and making new friends. Their sexual energy is undeniable and contagious, so they attract lovers quickly —keeping them for the long term is another story.

They possess inherent courage, determination, and drive toward their goal. Their hidden power lies in their ability to initiate change fearlessly, inspiring others to follow suit and take bold steps in their future and lives.

Aries must learn to give enough time and effort to people they care about, and recognize and respect their feelings and opinions. Learning to turn down the speed and volume of lashing out and to keep family and friends close for the Long-term goals are a great asset to this fiery sign.

CHAPTER 1
ARIES

INTERIOR DESIGN STYLE

As a Cardinal fire sign, Aries people are passionate, energetic and driven with a wide range of interest in flair and style, which explains why the Eclectic Interior Design Style is a great option when designing a space for Aries people. They thrive in a vibrant social atmosphere.

An entire wall dedicated to Aries's most daring photos and awards dresses the space with an uplifting mood, reflecting the personality of this passionate, fiery sign.

It is a dynamic twist to have furniture on wheels that can be rearranged on a whim. Aries can reconfigure their space in a heartbeat whenever inspiration (or boredom) strikes.

A designated corner for Aries' favourite inspirational quotes can be a great niche wall to draw motivation from: "Life's short; buy the shoes!"
Install an interactive mirror that gives motivational pep talks when Aries looks into it. "You've got this, superstar!"
An area rug resembling a treasure map will remind them of their adventurous spirit whenever they walk across it. The goal is to create a space reflecting Aries' vibrant personality and adventurous spirit while adding a lighthearted touch of humour.

CHAPTER 1
ARIES

Aries are bound to reflect their energetic, dynamic, and adventurous personalities. They are known for their boldness, passion, and desire to take on new challenges anytime. Expressing Aries's passionate, energetic approach to life and physical and intellectual stimulation is necessary when designing for Aries.

Aries people treasure their unique, non-matched flair of Self and feel comfortable with their sexuality. They are thrilled to experiment with their unique collectables, even sexual or sensual yet artistic pieces representing their self-indulging, unapologetic taste for provocative life and art.

Eclectic Interior Design Style subconsciously represents distinctiveness and non-conformative freedom, perfectly aligning with Aries's personality. Unconventional abstract art is fantastic for awakening Aries's curiosity and provoking a more profound way of thinking.

Create a focal point in the room that captures Aries's attention and is a source of inspiration. This could be a dramatic fireplace, a statement wall, or a bold piece of furniture that commands attention.

Lighting, which also represents the fire element, plays a crucial role in setting the mood and atmosphere of the space. Incorporate dynamic lighting solutions like adjustable fixtures, dimmer switches, and layered lighting to accommodate Aries' ever-changing mood and energy levels.

CHAPTER 1
ARIES

Incorporating asymmetry in interior design superbly aligns with Aries Cardinal's attributes of a curious and busy intellectual mind. Combining various styles of furniture and accessories is a great way to showcase Aries's non-apologetic, individualistic personality.

A modern downtown condominium furnished with a mixture of antique to mid-century modern furniture, dressed with fabrics of colourful tribal patterns embellished by provocative art, drawing sexual attention, is an excellent example of a match made in Heaven for an Aries home.

Aries people are open to mixing styles from modern to traditional Mid-Century and contemporary to Eastern styles of the ancient world. Almost every piece becomes a focal point. They are grabbing Aries's intellectual attention and feeding their intrigue, searching for the next inspiration or artistic pleasure in life.

Aries is proud of owning their sexuality. Bedrooms are of primary importance when designing or decorating a home. Luscious fabrics for bedding, draperies, and rugs are essential, especially if a partnership and lust are missing. Incorporating these applications sends unconscious messages of support to attract the perfect partner and more passion when needed.

CHAPTER 1
ARIES

COLOURS

Successfully decorating an Eclectic Interior Design Style with colours for a passion-driven Aries is quite a task. Attention-grabbing, vivid colours representing fire and a dynamic atmosphere become the main focus to keep the overall design style energetic and exciting.

Aries is a dynamic fire sign surrounded by shades of reds, oranges, yellows, and purples representing the fire element, exotic alignment, and decorating for Aries. It sends subliminal messages of fiery passion, unapologetic presence of sexual energy, intellectual imagination and creativity. Selecting and applying these powerful colours on the scale is imperative to avoid and promote conflicts or arguments.
Complementary colours of crips whites and light greys signifying the air element and enhancing Aries's office space can awaken intellectual creativity and improve productivity if they feel sluggish.

Aries individuals are drawn to vibrant and bold colours that reflect their energetic spirit and ignite their enthusiasm and vitality in life. Incorporating these design elements creates an interior space that resonates with the fiery spirit of an Aries individual, fostering a sense of passion, excitement, and adventure in their home, personal space, or environment.

CHAPTER 1
ARIES

FENG SHUI

Feng Shui is an ancient Chinese practice that emphasizes arranging your environment to promote harmony and balance. Here are some Feng Shui recommendations tailored explicitly for Aries individuals to help align their living space with their energetic and dynamic personality:

Integrate bold and vibrant colours like red, orange, and yellow to resonate with Aries's passionate and dynamic nature. However, avoid excessive use of these colours to prevent overwhelming energy.
On the contrary, if you have too many fire elements in your space, balance the Fire element with Water, Wood, and Metal elements. Incorporate shades of white, blue, green, metal, and wooden décor to create balance and harmony within the space.

Constant decluttering and an organized room are crucial for Aries, as their patience in looking for items might be triggering their short-tempered nature. Incorporate closed-in storage solutions like wicker baskets that are easy and convenient for "hiding" items when not in use. Introduce wood elements, such as plants, that make the space feel calm and grounded. Keep the environment organized and streamlined for clear thinking and energy flow that aligns with Aries' impulsive and fiery nature.

CHAPTER 1
ARIES

Open up the space to natural light and fresh air whenever possible. Aries thrive in well-ventilated areas that promote vitality and positivity.

Incorporate mirrors and reflective surfaces to amplify energy and create a sense of expansiveness. Place mirrors strategically to bring in more natural light and activate the stagnant areas of your space.

Decorate the room with dynamic shapes, such as a Pyramid shape, triangles, and angular pieces, to enhance Aries's active fire energy.

Fabrics of triangular and zig-zag patterns with fiery, bold colours can energize a room and add movement to areas of your home. It is a fantastic way to lift the mood of the space and ignite passion for life.

Showcasing images of the favourite destinations and decor pieces collected on adventures and explorations can kindle Aries's thrill for excitement and re-live their precious memories.

CHAPTER 1
ARIES

Physical activities and exercise are necessary for Aries, and they can significantly benefit from a dedicated workout corner that aligns with their energetic personality and lifestyle.

Living plants cleanse the air and bring fresh energy into the room, creating a calming atmosphere and helping the fiery nature to be more calm, peaceful, balanced and grounded. Aim for resilient plants that thrive with minimal care.

Aries people quickly start chores or projects, but still need to finish them. They tend to rush things or tend to butt heads with loved ones, which is a vital sign of having "too much" fire.
An excellent Feng Shui remedy is to apply indoor water features or a fish tank to soothe the nervous system and calm unpleasant attention within the space.

Feng Shui is about creating harmony and balance in your surroundings. These are some basic recommendations when
Applying Feng Shui for the zodiac sign Aries.

The goal is to create an environment that balances your energetic and passionate nature, offers a grounded and peaceful space that supports your well-being and strengths and encourages personal development and growth.

CHAPTER 2
TAURUS

Meet Taurus, the absolute Queen or King of comfort. If life were a couch, they would be the plushest, most cushioned one, and they've probably already claimed it as their throne.

Taurus folks take life at their own pace – slow and steady. You'll find them sauntering through the park, stopping to smell every flower along the way, and then lounging under a tree for the afternoon. Regarding change, let's say that Taurus approaches it with slow enthusiasm. They prefer to stick to their routines and surroundings.

Taurus is all about catering to their senses, including all five. They are the true connoisseurs of feeling, touching, tasting food and drinks and anything pleasurable. If there is a way to turn a dish into something warm, cheesy, and satisfying, Taurus has perfected it. The Charcuterie board has to overflow with colourful foods, nuts, truffle cheese, and figs, and be glazed with ice-wine jelly, paired with the perfect Pinot Blanc. They probably also invented loveseats with a luxurious faux fur throw or snuggle blanket. Indulgence is the key to life.

Taurus love their material possessions more than life itself. They are the masters of creating stylish, cozy nooks and comfy corners. So, if you ever need a chill buddy who brings the best snacks and has a sixth sense for finding the most relaxing spots in town, look no further than your friendly peer, Taurus.

CHAPTER 2
TAURUS

PERSONALITY/ELEMENTS/ RULING PLANET

Taurus is the first earth sign of the zodiac and values comfort, beauty, luxury and the realm of aesthetics, love, and relationships.

The Taurus season begins on April 20 and ends on May 20 as the spring advances, and the planting cycle starts in the Northern Hemisphere as the fall and harvest continue in the Southern Hemisphere.

Taurus is the second sign of the zodiac, representing the Bull, the celestial spirit animal, mirroring the second house's assets, possessions, personal values, and finances in Astrology. Surely, you have heard the phrase "Bull Market" or have seen the "The Bull Statue" on Wall Street. Taurus signifies money, the monetary system and the overall financial world.

Taurus's ruling planet is Venus, which explains why they admire and indulge in luxury, elegance, and style and love the finer things in life. They embody the Yin and female energy (regardless of gender) and aesthetics. They enjoy sensory experiences and appreciate the beauty of the natural world.

Taurus is known for its sensual and tactile nature, with Venus being the ruling planet. They thrive on physical pleasures, including touch, taste, and scent. And enjoy indulging in sensory experiences.

CHAPTER 2
TAURUS

Taurus people are grounded and are known for making sensible decisions and finding practical solutions to challenges. Taurus is the embodiment of patience. They're the ones who can wait in the longest lines without breaking a sweat, and they have the endurance to
See long-term projects through.

The reliable Taurus is the rock everyone can always count on. Their dependability and loyalty make them trustworthy, long-term friends, partners, and team members. Determination can sometimes lead to stubbornness, which is not easy to change. Once Taurus sets their sights on a goal, they become like a bull with a target in sight. Taurus believes in putting in the effort as long as it takes to achieve its goals.

Their tenacious, solid work ethic and dedication ensure they excel in completing projects and whatever they commit to. They have unwavering persistence and determination and are willing to work hard to achieve what they desire.

Taurus has an affinity for material possessions and enjoys being comfortable and contented. They appreciate quality and are often drawn to items that provide a sense of luxury with a grounded nature.

CHAPTER 2
TAURUS

Taurus has a practical, down-to-earth, and peace-loving demeanour. They're not ones for flights and genuinely dislike confrontations. Despite their strong exterior, Taurus is gentle, nature-loving and kind-hearted. They sincerely care about animals' welfare and saving the environment. They adore trusted friends and family and the security of their home, and often go to great lengths to ensure their loved one's well-being.

A routine-oriented Taurus finds comfort in familiar, everyday normalcy, stability, and accountability and prefers to keep their feet planted and grounded. They're creatures of habit and ethics, and appreciate predictability.
Taurus is one of the most resourceful, pragmatic, and savvy in focusing on the practical aspects of any situation. They have a "get things done" attitude and tenacity, making them reliable problem solvers.

As a fixed sign, Taurus has a tenacious nature, commitment, and loyalty in relationships and is a devoted and steadfast partner. They are persistent, value stability and long-term connection, and are willing to invest time and effort into their relationships. Often has the patience to work through challenges and obstacles, sometimes even longer than needed.

CHAPTER 2
TAURUS

INTERIOR DESIGN STYLE

Venusian energy is often associated with a strong appreciation, a keen eye for aesthetics, and a love of the beauty of all forms. That makes them well-suited for careers or hobbies that involve flair and interior design.

They are attracted to art, music, style, and luxurious surroundings that cater to their senses. This Yin/Feminine (non-gender specific) energy naturally gravitates toward visually pleasing environments with material comfort and security, a desire for financial stability
and enjoying the finer things in life.

This sensual earth sign often considers how a space feels, primarily due to its highly sensory nature. It may incorporate soft and luxurious fabrics, comfortable furniture, and soothing lighting
to create a tactile and sensory-rich experience.

As an earth sign, Taurus has grounded and practical characteristics that are an asset and perfect alignment when designing a Rustic Interior Design Style. They strive to create spaces that are not only beautiful but, most importantly, practical, functional and comfortable for their home and loved ones.

CHAPTER 2
TAURUS

A Rustic Interior Design Style is timeless, classic, and elegant and is the perfect interior design for the nature-loving, grounded, and artistic earth sign. Taurus has a practical, detail-oriented, down-to-earth, and peace-loving demeanour. They may meticulously select every element in a room, from the furniture to the accessories, ensuring that everything works together cohesively, leading to a well-thought-out, practical, and polished space that reflects their natural flair for interior design.

Taurus is an earth sign with a deep connection to nature, so Taureans may use rustic or traditional accessory choices using natural materials, reclaimed wood accessories, earth-tone colours, and incorporating elements of nature into their design.
They often value quality over quantity and are more likely to invest in high-quality, environmentally conscious furnishings made by local craftsmen and materials that will last rather than opt for cheaper, disposable alternatives that pollute the earth.
Taurus individuals can be resistant to change. While this trait can contribute to the stability of a design, it may also make them reluctant to update or modify their space as time goes by and life circumstances change.
And updates are needed.

CHAPTER 2
TAURUS

Taurus's Venusian influence and traits of beauty can make them skilled and environmentally conscious, thoughtful interior designers who create spaces that are not only beautiful but also functional and enduring. Their love of beauty, attention to detail, and practicality using timeless furniture pieces made of teak wood shines through in their design work, and their respect for nature.

Focus on creating inviting and comfortable living spaces with earth-tone palettes, oversized, plush furnishings, faux fur throw pillows, and soothing natural fabrics like cotton, linen and silk. Incorporate large, live plants into every room; they clean the air, bring fresh energy, and represent prosperity that Taurus people thrive on.

Taurus is known for its determination and patience. Design projects often take time and may face many challenges, yet they are one of the signs that are more likely to stay committed and see a project through to completion. This feminine energy (non-gender specific) earth sign is associated with financial stability and material comfort. This trait can be advantageous when working with clients on budgeting and resource allocation for interior design projects.

CHAPTER 2
TAURUS

COLOURS

When designing an interior space for an earth sign, Taurus tends to blend colours and colour palettes that reflect this earth sign's nature and the appreciation for comfort, beauty, and a sense of grounding.
Consider incorporating earthy colours like shades of taupe, beige, sandy tones, warm browns, and terracottas to create a warm and
a welcoming atmosphere and a cozy environment.

Taurus people often seek a sense of calm and tranquillity in their surroundings. Creamy whites and off-whites can create a serene and harmonious backdrop for the room and keep the atmosphere light, airy and inviting. Natural wood tones, from light oak to rich walnut, can add warmth and
a connection to nature.

Venus, the planet of love, beauty, and money, rules Taurus. Soft, muted, fresh grass greens can capture the feel of nature's spring beauty. Sage green, olive green, or mossy green can bring a soothing and serene vibe to the interior, reminiscent of lush landscapes.
The secondary colour palette of vivid turquoise to the regal sapphire blues represents the water elements that are complementary for this earth sign and are perfect accent colours for rugs, accent furniture or decor pieces that evoke balance and connection to the natural world.

CHAPTER 2
TAURUS

FENG SHUI

Feng Shui is an ancient Chinese holistic practice that considers the energy flow in a space and its impact on the individual's life. Incorporating these personalized elements and tailoring Feng Shui practice to a Taurus's unique preferences and characteristics can help create a harmonious and supportive living environment that aligns with their desires for comfort, beauty, and stability.

Taurus people appreciate a sense of balance and harmony in their surroundings. In Feng Shui, balance is achieved through the Bagua, an energy map that divides a space into nine different areas representing various aspects of life. Applying the Bagua Map and practices ensures that each location is well-balanced to create harmony in the space, aligning with Taurus's desire for equilibrium in life.

Taurus is an earth sign, so incorporating natural elements like wood, stone, and earthy colours is essential. Wooden furniture, stone countertops or accents, and earth-toned colour palettes can help create a grounded and nurturing atmosphere.

They value comfort, so they choose practical furnishings. Plush sofas, cozy rugs, and tactile textures like velvet or chenille can make the space feel luxurious, homey, inviting, and relaxed.

CHAPTER 2
TAURUS

Attention to sensory experiences is a must for Taureans. Soft lighting, scented candles, essential oil diffusers, and the fire element in Feng Shui will evoke passion, and soothing sounds can enhance the sensory aspect of the environment, which Taurus individuals value incredibly.

The Venusian trait appreciates beauty and grounded luxury, incorporating sentimental art and decorative elements that resonate with their aesthetic preferences. Highlight Taurus's appreciation for beauty by selecting artwork and decor that resonates with their aesthetic preferences. Encourage the displaying of beautiful art, sculptures, or decorative pieces that evoke a sense of beauty and serenity.

Make the most of natural light (representing the fire element in Feng Shui). Ensure that windows are unobstructed and that curtains or blinds allow for easy adjustment of light levels. Taurus individuals often enjoy spaces that are bright and sunny, well-lit and airy.

Invest in a comfortable mattress, high-quality bedding, and blackout curtains to ensure restful sleep and create a relaxing and nurturing bedroom tranquil retreat and environment that supports Taurus's placid nature.

CHAPTER 2
TAURUS

Taurus values organization and dislikes clutter. Promote a sense of order by incorporating effective storage solutions and decluttering regularly. Encourage using practical, multi-purpose storage furniture (coffee tables with drawers) that combines function and aesthetics.

Choose a colour palette that balances earthy tones with soft blues, signifying the water element, and greens representing the wood element, which are soothing colours to complement and balance a harmonious atmosphere.

Incorporate indoor plants representing the wood element, bring nature's calming and grounding energy indoors, and place them strategically throughout the home—the more, the merrier.

Encourage personalization by allowing the Taurus individual to display cherished possessions, family heirlooms, or sentimental items with special meaning.
These personal touches can enhance the sense of comfort, belonging, and security in the space.

CHAPTER 3
GEMINI

The zodiac signs of Gemini are known for their flamboyant, fun-loving, dual personalities. They're like having two personalities for the price of one. One minute, they're a social butterfly, the life of the party, and the next, they're off in their world, pondering the meaning of life with their curious mind.

Geminis are the kings and queens of multitasking; they can chat on the phone, answer emails, and bake a cake simultaneously. But ask them to decide, and you might as well be waiting for a snail to break the sound barrier.

Their minds are like a treasure trove of random facts and useless trivia. Need to know the capital of Zimbabwe or the history of the paperclip? Just ask a Gemini; they've got you covered.

When it comes to communication, Geminis like walking and talking to people. They'll keep you updated on every gossip, scandal, and conspiracy theory under the sun. It's okay if the
The story changes every time they tell it.

In love, Geminis are like a box of chocolates - you never know what you'll get. One day, they shower you affectionately, and the next, they give you the cold shoulder faster than you can say 'mixed signals.'

CHAPTER 3
GEMINI

PERSONALITY/ELEMENTS/ RULING PLANET

Geminis are generally light-hearted, happy, highly social people, born between May 21 and June 20 of each calendar year as late spring progresses into early summer.

Gemini is Astrology's first air sign, representing curiosity and inquisitive minds, and the third house of communication, short-distance travel, and siblings in the zodiac wheel.

This bubbly, Yang/Male (non-gender specific) active energy transitions spring into summer. Geminis can sometimes be inconsistent and ungrounded, accumulating and entertaining ideas from different angles due to the quick and reactive thinking patterns of their minds.

The fast-paced Mercury is the ruling planet for Gemini. Communications and media, education and curiosity, and highly intellectual minds are the most valuable traits of Geminis. They love learning, searching for answers, interacting and communicating with like-minded people.

Gemini represents the third house of learning, communications, short-distance travel, and siblings on the zodiac wheel, which resembles and are renowned for its excellent communication skills. They are naturally sociable, witty, and charming, making them adept at networking and forming connections.

CHAPTER 3
GEMINI

Gemini is a mutable sign, represented by the Twins in astrology, symbolizing their dual nature and energies. Geminis often exhibit two sides to their personalities, making them adaptable and versatile.
As the twins' sign in the zodiac, Geminis have "two sides" of the same person. One side is severe and extremely curious, and the other is Guffy, fun-loving and extraverted, feeling comforted in receiving attention from others.

Geminis are very social, highly intellectual, and ever-changing, transformative people. They are always looking for the next best thing in life, and it is hard to tie them down.

As the first mutable zodiac sign, representing adaptability, and twin's sign, they constantly "fight" their inner 'duality' and their dialogue within themselves. So, they often change their mind at the last minute and
Do not always consider others in their decisions.

Gemini gets bored quickly, and one must be extremely patient if married or have a family member, friend, co-worker/boss as a Gemini. Their intellectual mind is like a pool of whirlwinds. One day, they are here, next day, they are gone, but on the whole, their mind works fast.

CHAPTER 3
GEMINI

Geminis are known for their quick thinking and agility of thought. They can quickly grasp complex ideas and concepts.
Geminis are often skilled problem solvers.

Geminis have high energy levels and can become easily bored if not mentally stimulated. They thrive on variety and often seek out new experiences and challenges.

Geminis have a playful and mischievous side that makes them enjoyable. They use their charm and wit to entertain and engage others.

Geminis are keenly interested and naturally questioning of the world around them. They may ask numerous questions to gather information and form their own opinions. Due to their curiosity, Geminis can become easily distracted by new ideas and opportunities, changing their minds on the topic, sometimes leading to difficulties with focus and follow-through.

Geminis are often open to adventure and adore short or long-distance travels and new experiences. They desire to learn about cultures, seek out a variety of hobbies and activities and explore and try new things in life.

CHAPTER 3
GEMINI

INTERIOR DESIGN STYLE

Geminis are naturally curious as an air sign and carry the "thinking outside the box" mentality. The simplicity and intellectual attributes of the Industrial Interior Design Style are an excellent match for designing a space for this zodiac sign's intellectual mind and attributes.

Designing an interior space for a Gemini considers the dual nature of the grave, quick-witted, intellectually curious mind, and playful youth and child-like personalities that appreciate creativity. Imagine a pair of super-modern accent chairs echoing the cerebral mind and an antique, whimsical side table in the corner, signifying creativity and playfulness.

Pictures exposed brick walls showing the old-world taste, combined with modern art or a mixture of contemporary picture frames representing the duality of old versus new. No limit is too high to create a free-flowing, contemporary, Industrial Interior Design Style home for this sign that thrives on inquisitiveness, a liveliness that constantly changes.

This mutable Air sign adores social gatherings and entertaining friends and family, and is an excellent host; he enjoys having fun and celebrating. Considering these attributes provides a fantastic opportunity to create a space for socializing, adding a focal point in a room to showcase a "Conversational" piece of art that gets the dialogue going.

CHAPTER 3
GEMINI

Create multifunctional rooms or areas within the home to cater to Gemini's love for versatility. For example, a home office can also serve as a creative space or a guest room with a fold-out sofa for hosting friends.

Gemini is the first air sign in astrology and often enjoys open, airy spaces that allow for easy movement and free traffic flow. Consider an open-concept floor plan connecting the kitchen and dining area and a streamlined living room to accommodate and encourage entertaining, family, social gatherings, and easy traffic flow.

Mercury is the ruling planet of Gemini, the planet of communication, creating cozy conversation areas with comfortable seating arrangements for intimate talks. Geminis love to engage in lively discussions, so having an inviting conversation niche can be beneficial. Invest in flexible and adaptable furniture, such as modular furniture and sectional sofas that can be rearranged to suit different purposes or moods. Folding tables and chairs are also practical options when space is restricted.

Incorporate artwork and decor pieces that stimulate the mind. A well-organized bookshelf with various books, a study nook with a bulletin board for ideas and inspiration, or an art corner with supplies for creative pursuits can appeal to Gemini's intellectual curiosity.

CHAPTER 3
GEMINI

Incorporate decor items that reflect Gemini's duality. Consider wall art or decorative items that play with the twin symbolism to represent duality in nature.

Encourage artistic expression by dedicating a wall for artwork or creating a gallery-style display. Geminis may enjoy creating or displaying their art, so provide space for creative endeavours.

Incorporate sculptures and decor pieces that reflect change and movement. For example, use dynamic, bold, geometric patterns in fabrics, area rugs or draperies. Decorate with elements that reflect a sense of adventure and wanderlust. Consider incorporating travel-themed decor, maps, or globes to satisfy Gemini's curiosity about the world.

Geminis thrive in well-lit spaces. Maximize natural light with large windows and use layered lighting options, including task, ambient, and accent lighting, and metallic finished decor objects with reflective surfaces, to create a bright and inviting atmosphere.

Experiment with different lighting options. Install adjustable lighting fixtures, such as dimmer switches, to change the ambiance as needed. Blending natural, ambient and task lighting, floor lamps, table lamps, and pendant lights create mood and a variety of layered lighting.

CHAPTER 3
GEMINI

COLOURS

When decorating with colours for a Gemini individual, it's essential to consider their lively, adaptable, and dual-natured personality. Gemini is an air sign ruled by Mercury and tends to have a quick and changeable disposition.

Use shades of black, white, gray, charcoal, or neutral for walls, floors, and larger pieces of furniture to create a sense of balance and prevent overwhelming visual stimulation.

Create an accent wall using bold tone-on-tone dynamic wallpapers with geometrical shapes, perhaps reflecting metallic details. This can serve as a visual focal point and add excitement to the room, reflecting Gemini's lively, intellectual personality.

Geminis have a flair for the unconventional, and metallics like gold, silver and chrome can add a touch of glam and excitement to the decor. Consider metallic accents in furniture, light fixtures, or decor accessories.

Geminis appreciate intellectual stimulation, passion and fun, so incorporate the complementary fire element with creative decor pieces like metal finish candle holders or vibrant and lustful accent pieces of yellow, orange and red vases, bowls, accent cushions, and throws throughout the space staying within scales.

CHAPTER 3
GEMINI

FENG SHUI

Decorating a space for a Gemini while incorporating Feng Shui principles can create a harmonious and balanced environment that aligns with a Gemini. This air sign is ruled by Mercury, the planet of communication, and focuses on enhancing areas of the home associated with communication and social interaction.
The Bagua map places the communication area in the middle left section of the space. Decorate this area with communication symbols such as books, writing materials, or artwork that fosters dialogue and exchange of ideas that supports their mental stimulation, adaptability, and social nature.

Geminis appreciate versatility, so arrange furniture to allow for easy rearrangement. Contemporary, streamlined Modular furniture or lightweight pieces can be moved around easily and will suit multi-functional spaces and their nature of ever-changing needs. Reflect Gemini's dual traits by incorporating furniture and decor in pairs or using tone-on-tone colour schemes that have two similar contrasting colours, or a room with two distinct Industrial or Contemporary Design Styles.
Geminis are social butterflies, so consider creating several inviting gathering spaces in the home. Arrange floor plans and seating areas with soft, comfortable furnishings to make guests feel cozy and welcome.

CHAPTER 3
GEMINI

Feng Shui seeks to balance the energies of Yin/Feminine (passive) and Yang/Masculine (active). Incorporate both energies in the decor; pair soft, curved furniture (Yin) with angular or metallic accents (Yang).
Keeping the space clutter-free and organized is essential, as clutter can hinder energy flow and create mental chaos or blockage that Geminis may find unsettling and interrupting.

Display colourful and stimulating artwork or unique pieces representing the fire element and symbolically ignite passion and lust within the room. Select art and conversational pieces that feature intriguing topics to pique Gemini's curiosity, provoke discussions and engage their intellectual mind.

Live plants and green represent the wood element, growth, renewal, and change qualities that resonate with Gemini's adaptable nature. Incorporate fresh flowers, spring greens, and live plants to resemble spring and early summer, adding vitality and a sense of freshness to the space that connects to Gemini's youthful character.
It encourages Gemini's creativity by providing a display to showcase photos of cherished experiences, sentimental possessions or items that hold special meaning. This can help create an inviting, warm and personalized space.

CHAPTER 3
GEMINI

Display books, magazines, or educational materials in an organized and accessible way. Consider adding a bookshelf or a reading nook with good lighting to satisfy their intellectual thirst for curiosity.

Dedicate an area for creative pursuits, such as art, writing, or crafting. Ensure this space is well-lit and clutter-free, allowing for inspiration and exploration.

Geminis thrive in well-lit spaces, so maximize natural light by keeping windows unobstructed. Use sheer curtains or blinds to allow light to flow into the room while maintaining privacy.

If the Gemini works from home, create a flexible and dynamic area for a workspace that can easily be converted if the space is needed for other purposes. Invest in a comfortable chair and a versatile desk for focused work and collaborative projects.

By blending Feng Shui principles with a Gemini individual's unique intellectual characteristics, you can create an environment that supports their need for mental stimulation, adaptability, and social interaction while promoting a harmonious energy flow in their unique space.

CANCER

French Country Interior Design Style
Cardinal Water Yin/Feminine/Passive Energy
Intuitive Nurturing Emotional

CHAPTER 4
CANCER

The zodiac sign Cancer is like the sentimental, cozy Crab of the astrological ocean. They're the ones who have a tissue ready before
They even start telling a sad story.
Cancer is known for its emotional rollercoaster rides! Imagine crabs on a beach vacation – one minute, they're happily sunbathing, and the next, they're scuttling back into their shell because someone said
Something mildly upsetting.

Picture a crab carrying its house on its back; that's Cancer. They're all about that cozy, nest-building life surrounded by throw pillows, scented candles, and enough cozy blankets to supply a small army. These folks are proud of an ever-growing collection of sentimental objects and an unhealthy attachment to the tear-jerking movies they watch repeatedly.

They're the first to offer you a comforting bowl of soup when you're feeling down and the last to admit they're secretly binge-watching romantic comedies. The mysterious Crab secretly yearns for adventure but usually ends up in the comfort of their cozy shell, convincing themselves.
That staying in is the new going out.
So, suppose you ever need a friend who's an excellent cook, a great listener, and has the patience to help you find that missing sock you've been looking for.
Cancerian people will be that great friend.

CHAPTER 4
CANCER

PERSONALITY/ELEMENTS/ RULING PLANET

Cancer people are generally affectionate and passionate by nature. They prioritize protecting people they love and feel close to. As a water sign, this zodiac is an intense lover, a sensitive sign, which explains why they can be moody and stuck in the past. They are typically calm and chill until provoked.

According to Western Astrology, the zodiac sign Cancer begins on June 21 and ends on July 22. It typically covers the period from the summer solstice to past mid-summer in the Northern Hemisphere and late fall into winter in the Southern Hemisphere.

The astrological sign Cancer is the second cardinal sign on the zodiac wheel (starting a new season), marking the beginning of summer. The "cardinal" traits and characteristics are often known for qualities and the ability to initiate and take action. This is especially true for Cancer regarding emotional matters, home life, and family dynamics.

Cancer people are the first water sign on the zodiac wheel, carrying the traits of emotionally sensitive, caring, nurturing, and sometimes moody personalities. Cancerians have complex minds open to new ideas, but are also mysterious and complicated to read since they don't like showing their feelings. It is always a guessing game of emotions.

CHAPTER 4
CANCER

As the first water sign of the zodiac wheel, Cancer people are highly intuitive, sympathetic, and naturally gifted at reading people. They are always there for their friends and family, seeking deeper, long-term commitments. They don't do too well with flakes or obnoxious people.

The ruling planet of Cancer is the moon, representing our emotions and making the zodiac's most sensitive sign. Cancer signs are the best loving nurturers. However, sometimes, their caring nature becomes draining and overwhelming. It isn't easy to please a Cancer, even though they adore receiving passion and loving affection.

Cancer rules the 4th house on the astrological wheel, representing ancestry, the home and family dynamics. They tend to be the ones who take charge in family or domestic situations and are often seen as the emotional anchors in their relationships.

Cancer, as a Water sign, represents a Yin/Female (non-gender energy in astrology), one of the most emotionally sensitive signs in the zodiac. They are in tune with their feelings and the emotions of those around them. They often lead with their heart and can be empathetic and caring.

CHAPTER 4
CANCER

Cancers have a strong nurturing instinct. They excel at caring for others and are often family and friendship caregivers. They make great parents, friends, and partners because of their natural inclination to support and protect. While their sensitivity and nurturing tendencies are prominent, their cardinal nature gives them the drive and determination to create a supportive environment for themselves and their loved ones.

As a water sign, Cancers have a strong intuition and can often sense things without concrete evidence. This makes them great at understanding the needs and feelings of others. Loyalty is a paramount trait of Cancer individuals. They're dedicated and faithful once they form a solid emotional bond with someone.

As a cardinal sign, Cancer people can adjust to different situations and environments but feel most comfortable in a stable and secure setting. They often have a deep attachment to the past and may keep mementos and treasures with emotional significance.

Many Cancer individuals possess artistic and creative talents. They express themselves through various art forms, such as painting, writing, or music. Their home is essential, and they are dedicated to creating a warm and comfortable home environment for their families.

CHAPTER 4
CANCER

INTERIOR DESIGN STYLE

Decorating for someone with the Cancer zodiac sign involves creating a comfortable, nurturing, and emotionally supportive space. Cancer people are compassionate individuals who value their homes and families. Cancerian people love spending time at home. A comfortable home and a cozy environment are essential to this homebody type.

Design spaces that encourage relaxation and nurturing are paramount for people born under the zodiac sign of Cancer. A cozy meditation corner, a reading nook with a comfy chair, and a soft blanket create a calming, peaceful and nurturing environment.

With its conventional and classical traits, Cancer people are naturally drawn to timeless design and decor styles. The French Country Interior Design Style, with classical patterns resembling old-world and European flair and a welcoming atmosphere, is a "match made in Heaven" for this sentimental zodiac sign.

Traditional sectional sofas with upholstered, scrolled arms and plenty of practical and comfortable seats are an excellent choice for cozy family gatherings that Cancerians adore. Environmentally conscious selections of natural fibres, linen, and cotton reflect and align with this.
Nature-loving water sign of the zodiac.

CHAPTER 4
CANCER

Cancers love comfort and style. Blend comfortable, push and cozy throw blankets and soft faux fur cushions and textiles throughout the home. Think about a luxurious, silky, inviting chaise lounge and accent chairs with plenty of smooth, fluffy throw pillows to cuddle with. Invest in quality natural fibre bed linens, such as Egyptian cotton with high thread counts, for the bedroom.

As a water sign, Cancers are highly emotional and sensitive, often drawn to items with history and sentimental value. French Country Interior Design Style, embodying vintage or antique furniture and decor pieces, can evoke nostalgia and create a connection with the past that Cancer people value.
Rattan furniture is also great for bringing in the relaxing Southern or Seaside flair to match this water sign's natural traits.

Display family photographs and heirloom decor throughout the home. Family and heritage are paramount to Cancers, so celebrate these connections by creating a family wall or gallery to showcase these treasured images and memorabilia.
Choose art that tells a story or has personal significance. It might be artwork created by a family member, a painting that resonates with their emotions, or a piece that captures a meaningful memory.

CHAPTER 4
CANCER

Incorporate decorative, carved bookcases with open and closed shelving to stay organized with stylish storage solutions that blend seamlessly into the decor.
Hidden storage can keep the space clutter-free while maintaining a harmonious, peaceful, tranquil environment.
Personally hand-made crafts, DIY projects, or items with sentimental value and memorable touches throughout the room make the space feel unique and customized.

Given Cancer's association with the water element, consider incorporating beach or water-themed decor. Coastal artwork, seashells, and ocean-inspired items evoke a connection to the water element.
As the Moon is the ruling celestial body for Cancer, Moon-phase art, starry motifs, and semi-precious moonstones can be an Avant-Garde decor item and a powerful healing tool.

These are general guidelines, and each Cancer individual may have unique preferences. Creating a comfortable, emotionally nurturing, and harmonious environment is the key to decorating for this nurturing and emotionally sensitive water sign.

CHAPTER 4
CANCER

COLOURS

When decorating for the water sign, Cancer, choosing colours resembling water and oceanic themes evokes a sense of emotional connection and comfort; serenity is essential. Cancer individuals are deeply in touch with their emotions (representing water in astrology) and value their homes as safe, nurturing spaces.

Shades of soft turquoise blues and seafoam greens are calming and reminiscent of water, making them perfect choices for a Cancer's home. These colours generate an emotionally supportive and soothing atmosphere. Incorporating furniture, textiles and accent pieces with deeper shades of aqua turquoise and navy blues can be used as accent colours to infuse the space, add depth, and emphasize water elements in the room.

Soft apple-green, fresh grass, and moss-green represent the earth element and are a perfect complementary colour scheme for a nature-loving Cancerian home.

White can brighten up the space, adding a crisp and clean feeling. Creams and off-whites provide warmth and softness, creating an inviting atmosphere. Cancer is associated with the Moon, so accessories in celestial colours like silver are a great addition to resemble and enhance the Home's connection to this heavenly body.

CHAPTER 4
CANCER

FENG SHUI

Decorating with the ancient philosophy of Feng Shui principles and the Bagua Map for the zodiac water sign, Cancer, involves creating a nurturing and harmonious environment supporting their emotional sensitivity and intuition.

Cancer is deeply connected to the concept of home and family. The Bagua map places the family and community area in the left-center section of the space.
Enhance this area with decor that promotes security, comfort, and belonging, such as family photos, sentimental objects, and cozy furnishings.

From the five Feng Shui elements, fire, earth, metal, water, and wood, the zodiac sign Cancer is associated with the water element, so focusing on incorporating this element is imperative while maintaining a balance with other components.

Introduce water elements, such as glass, mirrors, water fountains, aquariums, or decorative bowls of water that represent the water element, and bring nurturing energy, a sense of flow and rejuvenation.
Place mirrors strategically to enhance a more open and inviting atmosphere.

CHAPTER 4
CANCER

Creating a balance between the two polarities of Yin/Feminine (passive) and Yang/Masculine (active) energies in the decor is essential. Blending traditional upholstered sofas and love seats with soft, organic patterns and fabrics (Yin/Feminine) and decorating coffee tables with straight-line metallic (Yang/Male) accent pieces, such as tall vases or tapered candle holders, is a great way to create a sophisticated flair in the room.

Cancer, as a water zodiac sign, and the ruling planet, the Moon, is also associated with the qualities of the Yin/Female (non-gender specific) energy. Like Cancer, feminine energy is inherently nurturing, always ready to provide love, care, and support to those in its circle. Their home must mirror the nurturing essence of their female (non-gender specific) energy.

This Yin/Female energy is closely linked to the cycles and rhythms of life. It influences the female menstrual cycle, tides, and Moon phases, and strongly affects the emotional cyclical nature of Cancer.

Both feminine energy and Cancer are strongly oriented toward home and family life. They place great importance on creating a safe and loving domestic environment and building close-knit relationships with family members. Cancerian feminine energy often has a profound connection to nature. Incorporating earth elements, such as warm, cane or wooden furniture and flooring, aligns with Cancer's nature-loving personality.

CHAPTER 4
CANCER

Select comfortable and inviting furniture with rounded edges and upholstered furniture that encourages relaxation and grounding connections, creating an "old world" feel to the home.

Design spaces like cozy dining areas and comfortable living rooms that revitalize family dynamics, enable larger gatherings and strengthen emotional connections and bonding. Use natural materials like wood and earthy textures to ground the space and reflect the connection to nature.

Display personal items, family photos, and heritage pieces throughout the home to add sentimental value and create a nurturing atmosphere. Keep the space organized and clutter-free. Use storage solutions that hide items while maintaining an open and soothing environment.

Incorporate plentiful living plants that nurture the Cancerian soul and bring growth and renewal energy into the home.

Feng Shui is about creating a balanced and harmonious living space. Adapting Feng Shui principles and focusing on creating an emotionally nurturing environment where Cancer people feel loved, secure, and supported is essential to developing a more holistic approach to design.

CHAPTER 5
LEO

The Leo personality is grand, majestic and dramatic. This zodiac is a natural-born stage diva and the life of every party! In Leo's world, everything is a stage; they're the lead actors. You can spot them a mile away because of their superstar dazzling charisma and Hollywood producer's ego. If you ever need someone to make an entrance, call a Leo. They'll arrive in a cloud of glitter and a fanfare of trumpets, even if it's just for a casual coffee date.

If you ever need to boost your ego, call your Leo friend. They're like the zodiac's personal cheerleaders, and they'll make you feel like the center of the universe. Remember to applaud and give them their
Well-deserved standing ovation!

Leos have a "roar first, ask questions later" approach to life. If you can't hear them coming, you need to listen harder! They have a knack for turning the most mundane stories into epic tales of heroism and are
never shy about taking center stage.

Their confidence is often mistaken for arrogance, but Leos are just practicing self-love professionally. They might secretly believe they're the universe's rightful rulers, but who can blame them when they're so charming?
So, in a nutshell, Leos are the zodiac's drama kings and queens, the rulers of the jungle (even if that jungle is just a suburban neighbourhood), and the ultimate party animals. Bow down to the Leo and
Get a VIP pass to their fabulous world!

CHAPTER 5
LEO

PERSONALITY/ELEMENTS/ RULING PLANET

Generally, Leos are confident, creative, and have natural leadership abilities, and it is associated with people born between July 23 and August 22. It is the fifth astrological sign, signifying the fifth house of creativity, art, children, romance and sexual pleasures in the zodiac wheel.

Leo is the second Fire sign of the natural zodiac wheel, representing the high peak of summer, which explains why their nature is so enthusiastic, dynamic, forceful, and sometimes hot-tempered.
The Sun rules the zodiac sign Leo in astrology, holding a central and commanding position as the life-giving force.
It shapes Leo individuals' core identity, vitality, and self-expression, actively seeks recognition and thrives in roles that allow them to showcase their talents and be recognized.

The Sun symbolizes the "ego," the conscious self, and the pursuit of personal goals in astrology. It reflects Leo's deep need for self-expression and a natural flair for the dramatic and artistic personality.
The Sun's active role as Leo's ruling planet contributes to their "centre-stage" and leadership qualities, and dynamic and charismatic personalities.

CHAPTER 5
LEO

Leo's intensifying qualities actively showcase their penchant for drama, amplifying experiences and expressions to command attention.
In their pursuit of self-expression, Leo individuals dynamically emphasize their achievements, passions, and charisma, creating a vivid and theatrical presence.
This active inclination towards exaggeration contributes to their vibrant personalities, making them stand out and seize the spotlight in various aspects of life.
Leo's excessive nature becomes a powerful tool for asserting their identity and leaving a lasting impression on those around them.
Leo is a confident Yang with (non-gender-specific) male energy. Their high charisma and enthusiasm make them natural leaders with a strong sense of self. Conversely, Leo's weakness is stubborn and self-centred arrogance.

Often, Leo magnifies their feelings, seeking attention and thriving on praise. They dislike being ignored or overshadowed, dealing with mundane tasks, or not being appreciated for their efforts.
Leos typically enjoy being the center of attention, expressing themselves creatively, and being surrounded by luxury and comfort. They have a warm and generous nature, enjoying the spotlight while being generous with their time and resources.

CHAPTER 5
LEO

Leo cultivates a deep passion for life, seeking experiences that resonate with their creative and expressive nature. They thrive in social settings where their charismatic and outgoing personality shines and infuses every moment with excitement.
Their passion is evident in their approach to challenges, where they embrace opportunities for growth and self-expression in the spotlight, seeking roles that allow them to showcase their talents and make a memorable impact. Their enthusiasm inspires those around them to adopt a more optimistic outlook.

Leo expresses their passion in relationships through heartfelt, grand gestures of love and a genuine commitment to creating extravagant memories and experiences. They appreciate life's beauty and make every day extraordinary through creativity and adventures, or by bringing passionate fire energy and warmth to their synergy.

The pursuit of joy marks Leo's passion for life, a celebration of individuality, and a determination to make the most of each moment. Their lively and enthusiastic approach creates a dynamic and uplifting atmosphere that leaves a lasting impression on those fortunate enough to share in their zest for life.

CHAPTER 5
LEO

INTERIOR DESIGN STYLE

Creating spaces and designing interiors for a Leo demands a deliberate infusion of luxury, drama, and an unmistakable sense of opulence.
A Leo's space is not just a room but a lifestyle.
The Hollywood Glam Interior Design Style is the perfect stage set where Leo's vibrant, confident, and theatrical personality takes center stage; whether it's an office or work room, a small art studio or a writing nook, having a space for self-expression is essential in Leo's environment.
The zodiac sign Leo's astrological connection reflects a lion's majestic quality in the animal kingdom. Animal prints and Faux fur signify Leo's fire element in astrology, mirroring underlying animalistic strength, magnetic sexual power and passion. Whether in area rugs, accent cushions, or artwork, these prints add a touch of the wild, symbolizing Leo's powerful personality and connection with their astrological sign.

Leo's home's regal and luxurious touches are intentional, echoing their inherent need for grandeur. Bold colours, sumptuous fabrics, and statement furniture pieces are aesthetic choices and deliberate expressions of their personality.
Leos actively seek to create an environment that radiates warmth, charisma, and a touch of extravagance,
even if they only have a small space to work with.

CHAPTER 5
LEO

Leos take immense pride in their homes as an extension of themselves, meticulously choosing elements that embody their confidence and distinctive style. Every piece of furniture, each splash of colour on the walls, and every decorative accent contributes to the narrative of who they are. Their homes become a canvas where they paint the story of their achievements, passions, and the very essence of their being.

The Sun, as Leo's ruling planet, is associated with the human ego, core identity, and vitality. The expressive nature of individuals born under this sign contributes to their dynamic and charismatic personalities. Everything in their lives is done on a sizable, larger-than-life, over-stated scale. Leo's achievements are not meant to be hidden but proudly showcased in their personalized decor, whether awards, certificates, or mementos, which become integral to the design, creating a space that celebrates their unique individuality and accomplishments, including their family and children. The personal touch is paramount in every detail, from monogrammed items to lavish, custom-made decor. A Leo's space is not just a reflection of their taste; it's an extension of their vibrant energy and expressive nature.

CHAPTER 5
LEO

Designing the Leo space is paramount to blending luxurious fabrics. Velvet, silk, and faux fur create a tactile richness that appeals to Leo's appreciation for the finer things in life. Upholstery, curtains, and pillows become not just functional but sensory indulgences.

Furniture and seating are not just about functionality but also about making a statement. Extravagant, stylish arrangements, such as large sofas or unique accent chairs, cater to Leo's penchant for hosting and entertaining.

The space is designed for a king of love of entertaining and to welcome and accommodate guests lavishly, fostering an atmosphere of celebration of intimacy, togetherness, and camaraderie.

Art is not an afterthought but a deliberate expression of individuality. Bold, vibrant statement pieces and large mirrors with gold or metallic finishes command attention. Every piece is carefully chosen to contribute to the overall sense of sophistication, making a lasting impression on Anyone who enters the space.

Lighting, as a fire element, is crucial in enhancing the theatrical ambiance of a Leo home. Elaborate chandeliers or distinctive pendant lights don't just illuminate the room; they cast a warm and dramatic glow that complements Leo's passionate and radiant personality.

CHAPTER 5
LEO

COLOURS

For Leo individuals, the world of interior design becomes a canvas to reflect their vibrant, confident, and theatrical personalities. Intense, igniting, "Fiery" colours create a space that resonates with Leo's animated character.

The warm tone of yellows signifies the Sun, Leo's ruling planet, bringing an uplifting and optimistic vibe to the interior that resonates with Leo's self-assured, positive outlook and adds a happy, cheerful touch atmosphere to the overall design.

Various shades of plush reds and regal purples are a signature choice for Leo's space and his appreciation for extravagance. Vibrant oranges inject playful energy into the design, creating a dynamic and inviting space that reflects Leo's creativity and lively, enthusiastic personality.

Gold accents signify the Sun, adding luxury and grandeur to the interior. Whether in furniture, decor, or accessories, gold complements Leo's desire for luxury and represents their regal disposition.
These colours not only exude supremacy but also symbolize vitality, resonating with the intense and passionate nature of a Leo and the deep sense of the majesty of this zodiac sign's surroundings.

CHAPTER 5
LEO

FENG SHUI

People born between July 23 and August 22 under the astrological sign Leo are ruled by the Sun, revealing radiating confidence, warmth, and an undeniable flair for drama, flamboyance, and grandeur.
Decorating a space for a Leo, a fire sign, with Feng Shui principles and the Bagua map involves creating a vibrant and luxurious environment that supports their boldness, creativity, and desire for admiration.

Leo individuals are often associated with fame, recognition, and leadership. The Bagua map places the fame and reputation area in the middle-back section of the space. Enhance this area with decor that promotes success, recognition, and visibility, such as awards, accolades, and artwork that reflect their achievements.

Embrace intense and vibrant colours that signify the fire element to ignite or enhance the fire energy in Leo's home or interior space. Lustful colours are foundational in designing a Leo-inspired space and selecting a palette that commands attention.
Opt for rich, warm colours like deep reds, luxurious purples, and dazzling golds to evoke the regality and passion that define Leo's extravagance and theatricality. These hues symbolize the lion's fiery nature and infuse a room with energy and vitality.

CHAPTER 5
LEO

Leo individuals have a penchant for luxury. Plush velvets, sensual satins, and faux fur also represent the fire element, adding a touch of opulence. Incorporating bold patterns such as animal prints also represents a fire element or geometric designs to amplify the room's visual interest and showcase.
Leo's passionate and forceful personality.

Leo's Yang/Male (non-gender specific) energy is associated with the fire element and is symbolized by this zodiac sign's firm, vibrant, and assertive characteristics. Feng Shui, ancient Chinese philosophy and practice, emphasizes the balance and harmony of environmental energies to promote prosperity, mental, physical and emotional well-being, and
Positive energy flow, Leo people flourish on.

Leo's Yang energy thrives in well-lit and open spaces. Ensure that natural light is maximized in living areas, and avoid clutter that may
Inhibiting the free flow of energy.

Use mirrors strategically to reflect and mirror light wherever possible, enhance brightness, and create a sense of expansiveness within the space.

CHAPTER 5
LEO

Integrate symbols associated with strength and royalty in the decor. This may include lion figurines, sun motifs, or other regal symbols representing Leo's majestic qualities. These symbols can serve as reminders of personal strength and resilience.

Encompass Leo's love for self-expression and individuality by incorporating personalized elements into the home decor.
Display achievements, awards, or items that hold personal significance prominently. This adds a touch of Leo's proud nature and contributes to a sense of personal empowerment.

Consider the Bagua, a Feng Shui energy map, to determine the optimal placement of Fire element enhancements within specific areas of the home. Aligning these enhancements with areas associated
With fame, recognition, and passion, it can further amplify the positive and dynamic attributes of Leo's Yang energy.

Consciously incorporating these Feng Shui principles creates a living environment that aligns with and enhances Leo's Yang energy, fostering a harmonious, energetic, and vibrant space.

VIRGO

Traditional Interior Design Style
Mutable   Earth   Yin/Feminine/Passive Energy
Analytical   Hardworking   Perfectionist

CHAPTER 6
VIRGO

Virgo, the practical, meticulous organizers, the detail-oriented wizards, the superheroes of colour-coded calendars. Virgo's home isn't just clean; it's a spotless sanctuary where even dust particles fear to settle because they will hear about it.

Virgo's perfectionist tendencies won't just plan a party; they'll design it according to the finest details. Every element is scrutinized, from the thematic colour of the napkins to the precise ratio of salsa to guacamole. If you ever need someone to proofread your life choices, find a Virgo, and they will be bold about putting their 10 cents in.

Virgos are notorious worriers. While enjoying a "carefree" day at the beach, your Virgo friend mentally calculates the SPF needed to protect you from harmful UV rays and packs a first aid kit and a survival guide.
In case the seagulls get too rowdy.
Virgos are the masters of mixed signals. They'll analyze every text message with the precision of a forensic scientist, but might appear calm.
When you ask them about their feelings.

Virgos are the opinionated yet settled heroes of the zodiac. They might drive themselves and everyone around them up the wall with their attention to detail. Still, we can't help but admire their dedication to practicality, living life with flair and a perfectly folded fitted sheet. Virgos are the true maestros of the mundane and the rulers of the meticulous!

CHAPTER 6
VIRGO

PERSONALITY/ELEMENTS/ RULING PLANET

Virgo individuals are naturally curious and observant, with keen analytical skills. They can dissect information, focusing on the finer details others might overlook. This systematic nature often makes them excellent problem-solvers and strategists.

Virgo people are born between August 23 and September 22, transitioning from the summer heat to autumn in the Northern Hemisphere and late winter into early spring in the Southern Hemisphere.

The constellation of Virgo symbolizes the Maiden, which represents the second earth sign, signifying the sixth house of work and daily routine, the health and pets of the zodiac wheel in Astrology. They thrive on calculating and setting big goals, and focusing on a stable, secure, and comfortable future is a priority, which is also one of the shared traits of others.

Earth signs they naturally get along with.

Mercury is the ruling planet, characterizing communication, fundamental education, intellect, and short-distance travel in astrology. Virgos are born skeptics, often opinionated, independent thinkers, notorious for overthinking and analyzing everything. They are acutely sensitive, but one would never know because they are also extremely good at hiding their feelings.

Virgos are masters of their love of meticulous order.

CHAPTER 6
VIRGO

Virgos are efficient, practical individuals who approach life with a grounded mindset. They prefer tangible, real-world solutions and are skeptical of overly abstract or speculative ideas. This practicality makes them reliable and trustworthy in various situations, a staple trait of an earth sign.

Mercury, the planet of communication and intellect, influences Virgos, contributing to their sharp minds. They enjoy engaging in intellectual pursuits, problem-solving, and continuous learning. Their curiosity and desire for knowledge drive them to explore various subjects.

Virgos are detail-oriented individuals who excel in tasks that require precision. They take pride in noticing the intricacies that others might miss. This attention to detail contributes to their success in professions that Please be sure to demand accuracy and thoroughness.

Despite their many talents and accomplishments, Virgos tend to be modest and humble. They don't seek the spotlight and often downplay their achievements. Their humility makes them approachable and easy to work with. Virgos are known for their sense of duty and responsibility. They take their commitments seriously and can be relied upon to fulfill their obligations.

CHAPTER 6
VIRGO

As an earth sign, Virgo transmits female energy that is naturally caring and nurturing; family always comes first. In relationships, Virgos are caring and supportive partners. They express their love through practical gestures and acts of service. Virgos are attentive to the needs of others, family, and loved ones and are willing to lend a helping hand when needed.

Virgo approaches relationships with a practical mindset. They value stability and are often realistic about the challenges that can arise. This practicality can reassure their partners, as Virgos tend to think through decisions and actions. Virgos pay close attention to the details of their relationships, remembering important dates, noticing subtle changes in their partner's mood, or planning thoughtful surprises.

This earth sign is hard-working, driven, and known for perseverance. They also tend to have high standards, making it difficult for others to please them. As a result, they get frustrated easily by incompetent people. This sign is not a pushover, and they avoid being lectured and will stand up for themselves. Virgo individuals value privacy and alone time and may need moments of solitude to recharge and fuel their mysterious and introverted nature. Virgo portrays a steadfast and trustworthy personality that many people are drawn to, whether in personal or professional relationships.

CHAPTER 6
VIRGO

INTERIOR DESIGN STYLE

Designing an interior space for a Virgo, an Earth sign known for its practicality and love for organization, can find harmony in the Traditional Interior Design Style. This style incorporates classic elements, symmetry, and a sense of order, aligning well with Virgo's grounded and detail-oriented personality.

Earth signs like Virgo flourish when surrounded by nature or nature-inspired objects in the design world. Non-pretentious, comfortable living is a must. Virgo loves everything to be extremely neat and organized, including their living or working space.

Go for classic and timeless furniture pieces that showcase pride in quality craftsmanship. With its elegant, organic lines and detailed carvings, traditional furniture resonates with Virgo's appreciation and respect for Mother Nature and environmentally friendly design style. Consider pieces like wingback chairs, tufted sofas, and antique-inspired tables. Reupholstered sentimental pieces are a conscious choice that an earth sign will value tremendously.

Traditional interior design style often emphasizes symmetry and balance. Arrange furniture in a balanced layout and use pairs of matching elements, such as side tables, lamps, or artwork. This approach appeals to Virgo's sense of order and aesthetics.

CHAPTER 6
VIRGO

Traditional interiors often feature rich velvets and classical fabrics in upholstery. Blend natural fibres, cotton, linen, and silk for sheers, draperies, Roman shades, or other window treatments and decorative elements. These materials warm the space, creating a comfortable and inviting home and atmosphere.

Consider wainscoting, crown moulding, and other architectural details and characteristics of Traditional design. As an earth sign, these elements appeal to a Virgo and add a layer of sophistication and visual interest to the room. Aligning with Virgo's appreciation for well-crafted details. Hardwood floors, reclaimed wood panels, and natural stone surfaces align with an earth sign. Avoid synthetic, artificial, cheaply made and low-cost bargain materials that are harmful to the environment and will not stand the time.

Integrate vintage accents and accessories to evoke a sense of history and charm. Vintage mirrors, ornate frames, or antique decor items can be strategically placed to add character and personality to the space. Design an accent wall with neatly grouped family photos and memorabilia. Traditional interiors often feature well-organized shelving and display areas. Invest in sturdy wooden bookshelves or cabinets with glass doors to showcase carefully curated collections and display items in an orderly manner.

CHAPTER 6
VIRGO

Choose classic and elegant lighting fixtures such as crystal chandeliers, brass sconces, or antique gold table lamps. These fixtures contribute to the overall ambiance of the space while maintaining a traditional aesthetic that resonates with Virgo's love for timeless design.

Create neat and functional workspaces catering to Virgo's perfectionism and practical nature. Incorporate a well-designed desk with ample convenient storage space, task lighting, and comfortable seating. Implement subtle organizational cues throughout the space. Labels, baskets, and storage bins can maintain order while blending seamlessly into the overall design and cater to Virgo's love for tidiness without compromising style. This dedicated workspace reflects Mercury's intellectual influence and aligns with Virgo's preference for organized and purposeful areas.

Combining these design elements forms an interior space that resonates with Virgo's practical and detail-oriented nature, provides a serene and harmonious, relaxing environment, and encourages productivity.
Embracing the Traditional interior design style and building a space harmonizing with Virgo's Earth sign characteristics provides classic and timeless surroundings for their practical and detail-oriented personality and lifestyle.

CHAPTER 6
VIRGO

COLOURS

Decorating and choosing colours for a Virgo, an earth sign, involves incorporating hues that evoke a sense of grounding, serenity, and sophistication. As an earth sign, Virgos resonate with colours inspired by nature.

Incorporating earthy tones such as neutrals, beige, taupe, and muted browns is Virgo's best friend. Shades of white and cream contrast a clean and organized backdrop, allowing other design elements to stand out. These neutral tones also enhance the sense of tranquillity and simplicity in the space. These Colours initiate a calming and grounded atmosphere, reflecting Virgo's connection to the astrological earth element.

Terracotta tones, reminiscent of baked clay, can bring warmth and a touch of Mediterranean charm to the space. Use terracotta as an accent colour in decor items like pottery, cushions, or small furnishings.

Soft greens, reminiscent of lush meadows and foliage, can add a touch of nature to the decor. Sage green or muted moss tones work well as accent colours, promoting balance and harmony within the space.

Infusing the space with warm earth-tone colours and a palette inspired by Earth's elements resonates with nature and shapes an environment that aligns with Virgo's practical and grounded personality.

CHAPTER 6
VIRGO

FENG SHUI

Dwelling deeper into decorating with Feng Shui principles and practices for a Virgo, an earth sign, involves creating a harmonious and balanced environment that aligns with Virgo's practical nature. Feng Shui, an ancient Chinese practice, emphasizes energy flow, or Qi (Chi), within a space to promote well-being and balance.

Utilize the Bagua Map, a Feng Shui tool that divides a space into nine areas, each corresponding to a different aspect of life. Place the Bagua over the floor plan of the home, or a specific room, aligning with the entrance, representing the life path and career area associated with the water element. Complementing Virgo's earth sign.

Strengthen the earth element in your decor by incorporating clay pots, ceramics, stones, or crystals. These items resonate with Virgo's earth sign and bring grounding energy to space. Place them strategically in the center or southwest areas, earth element sectors.
Embrace the Virgo preference for order by keeping spaces clutter-free. Clutter disrupts the flow of chi, and for Virgo, maintaining an organized environment is crucial. Regularly declutter and ensure that each item has a purpose, contributing to the overall harmony of the space.

CHAPTER 6
VIRGO

Strive for a balance of Yin and Yang energies within the home. Yin energy is passive and receptive, while Yang energy is active and dynamic. Virgo represents the Yin energy as an earth sign and often appreciates a balance between the two. Integrate soft, curved shapes (Yin) and more structured, angular elements (Yang) in your decor.

Choose furniture and decor from natural wood, stone, or clay. Earthy colours, such as browns, greens, and beige, resonate with Virgo's grounding energy. Use these colours in furniture, textiles, and wall colours to enhance. The earth element creates a soothing atmosphere.

Arrange furniture in the "command position" whenever possible. This means placing the bed or desk where you have a clear view of the entrance while being farthest from the door. This arrangement provides security and control, aligning with Virgo's need for practicality and order.

Use mirrors strategically to expand space and reflect positive energy. Place mirrors in areas that require more light or redirect the vital life force, Qi (chi). However, avoid placing mirrors directly facing the bed or any area that might create energetic disturbances.

CHAPTER 6
VIRGO

Virgos typically thrive in bright, well-organized workspaces. Ensure that desks are clutter-free, well-lit, and arranged to support productivity. Use organizational tools, such as filing cabinets or storage bins, preferably wood or natural materials, to maintain order in work-related areas. Wooden furniture and plants signify trees in decor, and the wood element in Feng Shui supports growth, flexibility, and positive energy flow. While Earth is the dominant element for Virgo, incorporating the wood element can bring conformity and enhance harmony.

Introduce gentle water features or representations of water, such as a fountain or artwork depicting water scenes. Water elements complementing the earth sign of Virgo heighten the energy flow, providing a sense of tranquillity. Place them strategically in the north, associated with the water element.

Feng Shui is about creating an auspicious, harmonious, balanced environment that works supportively with Qi and energy flow. It's a practice that involves mindfulness, intention, and a deep understanding of how the immediate environment and surroundings affect the psyche and how energy moves within a space. Blending these specific Feng Shui principles enhances the qualities of life that resonate with Virgo's earth sign nature and lifestyle and creates a comforting, aesthetically pleasing, and energetically supportive home.

LIBRA

Mid-century modern Interior Design Style
Cardinal / air /Yang/masculine/active Energy
elegant   charming   balanced

CHAPTER 7

LIBRA

The Libra's pursuit of perfect decor is the zodiac's eternal seeker of harmony and balance. Decorating for a Libra is like embarking on a cosmic adventure where every pillow, curtain, and piece of art must align perfectly, or the universe might implode.

Picture a Libra entering a room armed with a colour wheel, a Feng Shui compass, and a complex Pinterest board that rivals the Sistine Chapel.

Their pursuit of the perfect decor is nothing short of an epic saga. Like a stylish superhero, the Libra can spend hours debating the merits of a navy blue accent wall versus a serene shade of teal. "To rug or not to rug?" is a question that haunts their dreams, leaving them tossing and turning at night.

In the quest for a harmonious living space, the Libra faces the ever-present danger of "buyer's remorse." One day, the sofa symbolizes divinely inspired comfort; the next, it's the bane of their existence, and they're scouring online marketplaces for its replacement. It's a cycle as predictable as the changing of the seasons.

The Libra's love affair with decor, where throw pillows take center stage and curtain rods are the unsung heroes. In pursuit of the perfect aesthetic, they navigate online shopping, emerging victorious with a cart full of items that promise to transform their space into an oasis of equilibrium.

CHAPTER 7
LIBRA

PERSONALITY/ELEMENTS/ RULING PLANET

People born under the constellation of Libra between September 23 and October 22 are known for their distinctive personality traits, shaped by the influence of their planet Venus and their association with the element of air.

Libra is the seventh zodiac sign, represented by the symbol of the scales, balance and fairness. The seventh house represents partnerships and the significant other of the astrological wheel.
This cardinal air element channels a Yang/Masculine (non-gender specific) energy that exemplifies the beginning of autumn and the fall equinox, when the sun is exactly above the equator and the day and night are of equal length.
As an air sign, Libra is typically communicative with intellectual, curious minds.

Libra individuals are often associated with balance and harmony. The scales symbol represents their desire for equilibrium in all aspects of life.
They are known for their diplomatic and fair nature.
They have a strong sense of justice and seek to create a fair and balanced environment in their relationships and social interactions.
Libras value harmony and are skilled at resolving conflicts and finding compromises. Their diplomatic nature helps them maintain peace in relationships and group dynamics.

CHAPTER 7
LIBRA

Air sign people are perceptive with analytical minds. Libras are naturally born skeptics yet open-minded to new ideas to find their conclusion.
They are observant, taking notes on minor details. Libras are often intellectually inquisitive and enjoy engaging in conversations that stimulate their minds.
They love learning, searching for answers, interacting, and communicating with others.
They appreciate thought-provoking discussions and have a love for learning.
Libras are charming individuals. They enjoy socializing, forming connections, and maintaining relationships. They are well-liked, naturally attract others with their kindness and grace and can get along with people from various walks of life.
They are fun-loving, light-hearted, friendly and social people and are happiest when they put smiles on people's faces.

Libra people value long-term, meaningful relationships with deeper connections and do not like selfish people. A laidback, loyal friend and ally would rather lose a war than a valuable relationship.
Libra people do not like arguments and confrontations, and will forgive, but remember the betrayal.

CHAPTER 7
LIBRA

One challenge for Libras is a tendency towards decision-making. This is often linked to their desire to weigh all options, and finding the most balanced choice is challenging. Libras' desire for balance and fairness may cause them to consider options extensively and need help to make choices.
Fearing that they might upset others and the equilibrium.

Libra admires style, beauty, grace, and physical attributes. They appreciate the arts, fashion or other creative pursuits. Venus is the planet of beauty and love, influencing Libra's passion for exquisite and aesthetically pleasing things. These lovely, graceful, classy and flair-driven individuals have a natural eye for fashion and design. They respect nature, enjoy cultural experiences, and express themselves creatively. Libras might enjoy engaging in do-it-yourself (DIY) projects, whether crafting, home improvement, or any creative endeavour that allows them to express their flair and artistic side.

While not every Libra will exhibit artistic tendencies, many find satisfaction and fulfillment in creative pursuits that align with their beauty, balance, and harmony values. It's essential to remember that individual interests and talents can vary, and astrological traits provide general insights rather than strict determinants of personality.

CHAPTER 7
LIBRA

INTERIOR DESIGN STYLE

The influence of Venus, the ruling planet of Libra, plays a significant role in shaping the interior decorating style preferences of individuals born under this zodiac sign. Venus is associated with love, beauty, and aesthetics, and its subconscious influence often guides Libras toward creating visually appealing and harmonious living spaces.
Midcentury Modern Interior Design styles may resonate with Libras attraction to glamour, flair, and style.

Libras' classic elegance, under the influence of Venus, may be drawn to traditional and timeless design styles. Classic elegance often features refined furnishings and luxury. Rich fabrics, traditional patterns, and sophisticated colour palettes can create an enduring and graceful aesthetic.

Libras seek balance in all aspects of life and adore symmetrical furniture placements in their interior decorating style. They are likely to use an equal proportionate layout, placing furniture and decor items in a way that creates visual equilibrium.
This Venusian zodiac sign has a keen eye for aesthetics and may choose functional and visually pleasing decor. They may incorporate art, sculptures, and other decorative elements that echo a sense of beauty.

CHAPTER 7
LIBRA

Libras appreciate luxury and may incorporate elements of opulence into their decor. It includes high-quality fabrics, elegant furnishings, and tasteful accessories that add a touch of sophistication to the space.

People born under the scale appreciate nature and are attracted to nature-inspired items and Feng Shui principles, emphasizing balance and positive energy flow in a space.
They may arrange furniture and decor according to these principles to create a harmonious and inviting environment.
While Libras appreciate elegance, they also want their homes to feel inviting and comfortable. They may choose plush furnishings, cozy textiles, and warm lighting to create
a welcoming atmosphere for themselves and their guests.
They might display artwork, sculptures, or handmade items that reflect their creative side and contribute to the space's overall aesthetic.

Libras often pay attention to the small details that can enhance the overall design. This might include carefully chosen accent pieces, thoughtful arrangements, and well-coordinated accessories that contribute to the Overall balance and harmony of the space.

CHAPTER 7
LIBRA

Given their social nature, Libras appreciate friends, family and community. They may prefer a living space designed for entertaining and socializing with friends and family: Idealize floor plans of conversation areas, cozy nooks for intimate gatherings, and accommodating and encouraging interaction among loved ones.

As a cardinal air sign, Libras appreciate the flexibility to change and adapt their living spaces. They might prefer furniture that can be easily rearranged and decor items that can be mixed to keep the space fresh and dynamic.

While seeking balance, Libras may also appreciate the eclectic and free-spirited nature of the Boho-chic style, reflecting their fun-loving nature, mixing patterns, textures, and luxurious and harmonious materials. Selecting conversational pieces that depict social and philosophical themes forms a unique and intriguing atmosphere that is peaceful and intellectually stimulating, which Libra individuals value immensely.

Venus's love for natural beauty might inspire Libras to form an indoor-outdoor connection in their living spaces. Large windows, plants, and materials respectful to nature can bring a sense of the outdoors inside, fostering a harmonious, colourful, and serene atmosphere.

CHAPTER 7
LIBRA

COLOURS

When choosing interior decorating colours for a Libra, an air sign known for its balance, harmony, and appreciation for aesthetics, focus on creating a fresh, light atmosphere, an inviting, elegant, and well-balanced space. Venus, the ruling planet of Libra, naturally attracted classy and sophisticated colours. As an air sign, Libra's auspicious colours, such as white, neutrals, beige, ivory, and shades of luxurious grays, keep the interior welcoming, bright and luminous, signifying the air element and intellectualism. Warm charcoal gray adds depth and can be a contrasting backdrop for other bolder colours.

A complementary colour scheme of shades of lavender, lilac, pink, fuchsia, reds, burgundy, or marsala for more profound, intense colours denotes the fire element in astrology, which is favourable to air elements and aligns well with Libra's aesthetic sensibilities and Venusian influence. These colours evoke joy and passion, bringing intercity and excitement and modelling the Yang/Male (non-gender specific) energy in Feng Shui and astrology.

Tertiary colours of lighter blues convey a nurturing atmosphere and tranquillity, while earthy green tones, such as olive or forest greens, add a touch of nature, creating a calming, harmonizing and grounding effect to the interior, adding serenity and highlighting the graceful attributes of Libra.

CHAPTER 7
LIBRA

FENG SHUI

In ancient Chinese art, Feng Shui of symphonic energies in the environment aims to create a balanced, harmonious space that promotes well-being and positive energy flow. For a Libra, an air sign associated with balance and harmony, incorporating Feng Shui principles can enhance the clean and stylish Midcentury Modern Interior Design style and
The overall energy of the living space.
The Bagua square is a tool used in Feng Shui to map out specific areas and directions associated with various aspects of life to enhance the energy flow of the room. The area signifies relationships and partnerships in the Bagua map, which is in the farthest right portion of the space, aligning with the Libra zodiac sign that focuses on balance and interrelationships.
Blend colours like whites, creams, or soft, calming pastels to keep that specific space or corner light and airy, and introduce decor items that represent happy couples or partnerships, aligning with Libra's element of air and
their lust for balanced and harmonious relationships.
Blend sophisticated, classy colours of warm whites, soft, muted blush or lilac to create a soothing, serene and welcoming atmosphere. They enhance the relationship area on the Bagua map to restore, boost, and strengthen partnerships. Avoid overly bold or contrasting colours that may disrupt the balance and Libra's sense of sophistication.

CHAPTER 7
LIBRA

Since Venus rules the astrological sign Libra, which signifies passion, love, and beauty, consider painting and images depicting companionships or a bouquet of white flowers and infuse the space with rose or lavender incense to cater to all senses associated with the planet Venus. Integrate decorative pieces that symbolize love and balance, such as pairs of objects, romantic artwork, or items that represent the balance of yin and yang energies. Images of nature, serene landscapes, or artwork that feature balanced compositions are calming and infusing the space with auspicious and positive energy. Decorate with extravagant candleholders and coffee table interior design books in pairs, and luxurious decor pieces symbolize harmony and balance. Nature-inspired images of animals in pairs, romantic scenes, or representations of the natural world can enhance the nature-loving Venusian Libra energy and create a warm, loving and comforting atmosphere. Natural elements like plants bring the wood element in Feng Shui, representing flexibility, growth, and vitality. Place a bouquet of fresh-cut white or soft pink flowers or live plants in the relationship area to promote harmony and love. Choose plants with round or oval-shaped leaves to create a smoother, more Yin or feminine energy. The five elements of Feng Shui are fire, earth, metal, water, and wood. Incorporating each factor creates unity and tranquillity within the interior space.

CHAPTER 7
LIBRA

Good lighting is essential in Feng Shui, especially for an astrological air sign of Libra. Ensure the relationship area is bright, sunny and well-lit with natural and artificial light sources that provide a harmonious atmosphere. Avoid overly bright, harsh, blue artificial lighting, and use soft, ambient lighting for a cozy atmosphere. Strategically placed mirrors reflect natural light and create a sense of expansiveness. Mirrors also symbolize the water element that promotes nurturing in astrology and can intensify energy flow when placed thoughtfully.

Libras appreciate modern, open-concept, spacious design styles and balanced environments, value fairness and equality, and enjoy spending time with others. Arrange furniture for smooth, unobstructed pathways, avoid clutter, and keep spaces organized to promote free energy flow.
Arrange furniture symmetrically and in pairs to create a sense of equilibrium and create conversation areas that welcome social interaction to encourage intellectual conversations where everyone has an equal and Inclusive opportunity to share their thoughts.
Personal preferences play a significant role in Feng Shui, so adapting these principles to the individual's tastes and lifestyle is essential. Interweaving these ancient practices conceives a unique interior design style that aligns with Libra's personality, traits, and energy, creating an optimal balance in the home.

SCORPIO

Coastal Interior Design Style
Fixed   Water   Yin/Feminine/Passive Energy
Orderly   Mysterious   Loyal

CHAPTER 8
SCORPIO

Scorpios are the James Bonds of the zodiac, armed with charisma, mystery and an arsenal of emotions. The enigmatic Scorpio, the zodiac's mischievous undercover agents, always hover in the shadows with a grin, plotting the next adventure in their cosmic escapade. Scorpios don't just do things; they plunge into the pool's deep end with unbridled intensity and enthusiasm.

The infamous Scorpio sting. One moment, you're chatting about the weather; the next, you're caught in their verbal spiderweb. Scorpios have an uncanny ability to transform mundane conversations into intricate puzzles, leaving their unsuspecting conversation partners bewildered and questioning their reality.

On the outside, Scorpios may appear as calm as a cucumber, but beneath that stoic exterior lies a storm of emotions. Think of a Scorpio as a volcano: dormant for ages, but everyone better brace themselves when it erupts.
Let's remember their magnetic charm. Their charisma is as potent as a love potion, and one flash of that secretive smile could send even the most level-headed souls tumbling into the abyss of Scorpio enchantment.

When it comes to trust, Scorpios operate on a need-to-know basis, and guess what? You don't need to know their business, but they are open about getting into yours. Their secrets are like precious gems locked away in a vault guarded by mythical creatures. If you manage to unearth a Scorpio secret, congratulations, you've achieved the impossible, akin to discovering Atlantis or convincing a Leo to share the spotlight.

CHAPTER 8
SCORPIO

PERSONALITY/ELEMENTS/ RULING PLANET

Scorpio is a mysterious creature, the second water sign of the zodiac wheel. They are emotional, highly intuitive, compassionate, and naturally gifted at reading people, with deep feelings that one may never see on the surface. Scorpios are known for their intense and passionate nature. Whether it is love, work, or personal interests, they dive in wholeheartedly, often seeking deep, meaningful connections.

People born between October 23 and November 21 fall under the sun sign Scorpio, representing the eighth sign and the eighth astrological house of the zodiac wheel, which signifies shared resources, inheritance, the significant other's money, occults, transformation and deaths. The transformative Pluto is the ruling planet of Scorpio, which embodies karma, the meaning of profound unconscious transformation, and teaches us to let go of attachments and fear.

Scorpio people are genuinely committed zodiac signs. A mystery surrounds Scorpios' fixed water sign, which tends to keep their emotions hidden and guarded. As fixed signs, Scorpios are set in their ways, making it difficult for anyone to change their minds. This secretive nature adds to their allure. Scorpios experience emotions with great intensity. Their emotional depth allows them to connect profoundly with others, but they can also be prone to experiencing extremes, swinging between passion and intensity.
It is everything or nothing.

CHAPTER 8
SCORPIO

Scorpio people are fiercely competitive and do not allow anything or anyone to get in the way of achieving greatness. This zodiac is extreme, an intense lover, and can lose their temper when crossed, so watch out for the consequences. They can be vindictive if they feel betrayed.

Scorpios carry magnetic, intriguing auras with profound and complex minds. They are independent, naturally skeptical, and take their time opening up to others. This sign is a mysterious, hard-to-read personality that does not like showing emotions, often with significant trust issues and is always on guard.

As a fixed astrological sign, Scorpios are determined and resilient individuals. They can handle setbacks and challenges gracefully and regenerate like a phoenix rising from the ashes. Scorpios are known for their diplomatic skills. They can navigate complex situations tactfully and with poise, making them effective in leadership roles. Scorpios are decisive and unafraid to take calculated risks when faced with decisions. They are strategic thinkers and enjoy analyzing situations, probing beneath the surface, and uncovering hidden truths. Their keen observational skills make them excellent problem-solvers. A strong sense of justice drives Scorpios. They can be advocates for fairness and are not afraid to confront injustice. This trait aligns with their determination to bring about positive change.

CHAPTER 8
SCORPIO

Scorpios exude a magnetic charisma. Their presence is captivating, drawing others in with confidence, mystery, and a touch of intensity. With their mysterious nature, Scorpios can be charming and socially adept. They know how to navigate social situations with finesse, making them engaging conversationalists and often the center of attention. Despite their intensity, Scorpios can have a surprisingly sharp and witty sense of humour that they use to connect with others. Despite their often stoic exterior, Scorpios are highly sensitive and are deeply affected by emotions, both their own and others.

Scorpios carry a Yin/Female (non-gender specific) energy as a water sign. They are complex individuals with deep layers of emotions and conscious and subconscious thoughts. Scorpios are loyal partners. They invest deeply in their connections and expect the same loyalty in return. Betrayal can be particularly devastating for Scorpios.

Just as their ruling planet, Pluto, is associated with transformation, Scorpios undergo significant personal transformations throughout their lives. They embrace change and the opportunity for self-growth and renewal. While Scorpios value deep connections, they also cherish their independence. They appreciate having personal space and autonomy in their pursuits.

CHAPTER 8
SCORPIO

INTERIOR DESIGN STYLE

When choosing a design style for a water sign like Scorpio, it's essential to consider and focus on the water element, reflecting emotional depth, intensity, and nurturing qualities associated with Scorpio's astrological sign. Designing a Coastal or Seaside-inspired Interior Design Style involves merging the calming and fluid elements of nautical decor with the intense and mysterious qualities of the water sign. Embrace luxurious aesthetics with dark, intense colours like navy to create an eerie, intimate, and sophisticated atmosphere that reflects personal expression and aligns well with Scorpio's mystical characteristics.

Scorpios appreciate authenticity and a space that tells a story of their journey. Personalized coastal decor pieces featuring ocean scenes, aquatic life, or abstract representations of water hold sentimental value to the Scorpio individual. Display artifacts with darker tones or souvenirs from meaningful beach trips that add depth to the coastal theme that resonates with Scorpios' water element. Add a water fountain aquarium to promote a calm and collected atmosphere to connect with Scorpios' deep thinking and intuitive nature. Blend subtle nautical elements without overwhelming the space. Consider incorporating marine ropes, textured fabrics with nautical patterns, or driftwood decor. These elements nod to the coastal theme while maintaining Scorpio's preference for depth.

CHAPTER 8
SCORPIO

Design a private retreat space within the home by creating cozy reading nooks, meditation corners, secluded areas for introspection and a space for inner reflection. Scorpios appreciate having intimate spaces to recharge and connect with their inner selves and transformative experiences.

Decorate with seashells, the art of symbolic significance, like a phoenix rising, representing Scorpio's profound transformational nature. Integrate mystical and spiritual accents, crystals, tarot cards, or symbolic decor items that can add a mystery to the space that resonates with Scorpios' intriguing nature and interest in the occult and esoteric wisdom. Engage the sense of smell with scented elements reminiscent of the coast. Consider coastal-inspired candles or diffusers with scents like sea breeze, salt air, or ocean mist to Evoke a coastal atmosphere within the space.

Adopting smooth, refined natural and artificial lighting is essential to create an intimate and mysterious ambiance for Scorpios' space. Select crystal pendant lights or table lamps with darker shades that make the room feel calm and soothing, and add a luxury touch. Controllable dimmers can help adjust the lighting to suit different moods and occasions, fostering a tremendous sense of warmth, comfort, and security that this water sign values.

CHAPTER 8
SCORPIO

Integrate luxurious textures into the coastal decor. Opt for plush area rugs, navy blue velvet throw pillows, soft, cozy blankets, layered textiles with nautical motives, seaside-like patterns, and darker shades of blues or greens to bring in water and earth elements that are complementary for Scorpios. Luxurious and plush fabrics like silks, velvets, and faux furs represent chic elegance to Provide the cozy comfort for Scorpios' personalities to thrive.

Dark wood furniture and accent pieces bring superior flair, add warmth and depth to the coastal design, enhance the Scorpio colour palette, and add a sophisticated touch to the overall aesthetics. Select customized plush, comfortable sofas and chairs with dark upholstery or coastal-inspired patterns. Include ample seating arrangements to accommodate social gatherings, as Scorpios appreciate deep connections with others. Consider curved sofas, round coffee tables, or circular mirrors to enhance the space's overall harmony and easy energy flow. Incorporate statement furniture pieces that reflect Scorpio's classy personality.

Designing a Coastal Interior Design Style that blends nautical or seaside-like decor pieces and colours resembles Scorpio's emotionally intense and mysterious qualities.

It creates a private, mystical, safe and nurturing home that Scorpios treasure and appreciate tremendously.

CHAPTER 8
SCORPIO

COLOURS

When designing a coastal-inspired space for Scorpios, consider focusing on deeper shades of navy blue and darker olive or hunter-greens that align with the Scorpio personality and add a touch of mystery to the nautical design style. Forming a unique, captivating space, subconsciously reflecting a Scorpio energy, a water sign known for its emotional nature, psychological depth and intensity, passion and mysterious sensuality. Consider rich, sensuous navy tones reminiscent of the ocean's depth for personal bedrooms and accent walls, aligned with Scorpio's water element and transformative energy or nature.

Earthy hues like dark brown, olive, or hunter green provide grounding earth elements that complement Scorpio's water element and subconsciously aid Scorpio's constantly thinking and psychologically heavy mind. Muted neutrals, such as warm and soft beige or greys for larger surfaces, serve as secondary colour schemes connecting to the natural world and create a calming atmosphere in the space.

Lustrous, sparkling silver, pewter, nickel, black and charcoal accent pieces establish elegance and class, providing opulent reflective surfaces and enhancing the overall contrast and intensity of the Coastal Interior Design style. These metallic accents complement Scorpios' preference for timeless elegance, grace and luxury.

CHAPTER 8
SCORPIO

FENG SHUI

Designing a space for a Scorpio using Feng Shui and the Bagua Map involves aligning the energy of the space with Scorpio's intense, profound and transformative characteristics. The Bagua Map is an essential tool that divides a space into nine areas, each corresponding to different aspects of life, such as wealth, relationships, career, and health.

Scorpio is associated with the water element in astrology and Yin/Female (non-gender specific) energy in Feng Shui. Enhance the water energy in the North area of the Bagua Map to nourish and stimulate a nurturing and protective environment. Place water features like a small fountain or a fish tank, deep blue crystal decor items like blue topaz or blue tourmaline, or reflective surfaces like glass and mirrors.

The wealth area is located in the Southeast section of the Bagua Map and is associated with the wood element in traditional Feng Shui. To enhance the energy in this area, incorporate elements representing wood, such as healthy, live plants, wooden furniture, green, monetary symbols of growth, and coins aligning with Scorpio's astrological power of the eighth house of the zodiac wheel, representing birth, death, rebirth, inheritance and other people's money. Addressing this field is particularly important to enhance and attract prosperity and financial well-being, as Scorpio treasures their financial safety and security.

CHAPTER 8
SCORPIO

Create a balanced colour palette that reflects Scorpios' water element to aid their emotional mood swings and intense personality. Bedrooms, accent walls, and upscale decor in rich turquoise, royal and navy hues resembling water in nature align with Scorpio's emotional and nurturing personality. Use shades of warm caramels, chocolate browns, earth tones, or neutrals (signifying the Earth element in Feng Shui) to complement and balance these intense blue colours and avoid visually overwhelming the space.

Design and implement a harmonious furniture arrangement to ensure an open, unblocked energy flow through the space. Place key pieces strategically to foster a sense of connection and intimacy and nurture Yin/Female (passive) energy. Scorpios highly value their personal space and surroundings. Integrating symbolism resonates with Scorpio's transformative power. Be sure to exhibit artwork or decor items that symbolize the phoenix rising, scorpion, or other symbols of rebirth, reproduction, and regeneration. Personalize the space with meaningful items that tell a story. Decorate with symbolic items that resonate with Scorpios' spiritual and transformative nature. Scorpios appreciate meaningful possessions. Incorporate items with sentimental value, such as family heirlooms, personal artifacts, or items collected from travels. These personal touches add depth to the space and show Scorpios' admiration and values.

CHAPTER 8
SCORPIO

The west and northwest areas of the home on the Bagua Map signify the metal element in traditional Feng Shui. Combining mirrors or silver-coloured metallic elements like pewter, nickel or wrought-iron frames and decorative items enhances creativity and creates a luxurious surrounding. Silver also signifies the water element that aligns with Scorpio's astrological water sign, creative personality and nature.

Design private retreat spaces within the home, such as a reading nook or a private meditation corner, where Scorpios can recharge and connect with their inner selves. Honour Scorpios' need for privacy and intimacy by arranging furniture to create cozy and secluded spaces. Use intimate, mystical, and sensuous lighting to create a comfortable atmosphere. Consider using candles, string lights, or lamps with soft shades to form a sensual mood and ambiance. These lighting choices align with Scorpio's appreciation for mystery, privacy and intimacy and establish a cozy atmosphere. Consider using room dividers, curtains, or furniture arrangements that provide a sense of enclosure in the home. Regularly declutter and maintain a clean space to support Scorpios' appreciation for a peaceful home and need for structure.

These Feng Shui principles and aligning the design with the Bagua Map create a home that resonates with Scorpios' energy, fostering a peaceful and harmonious environment where Scorpio people thrive.

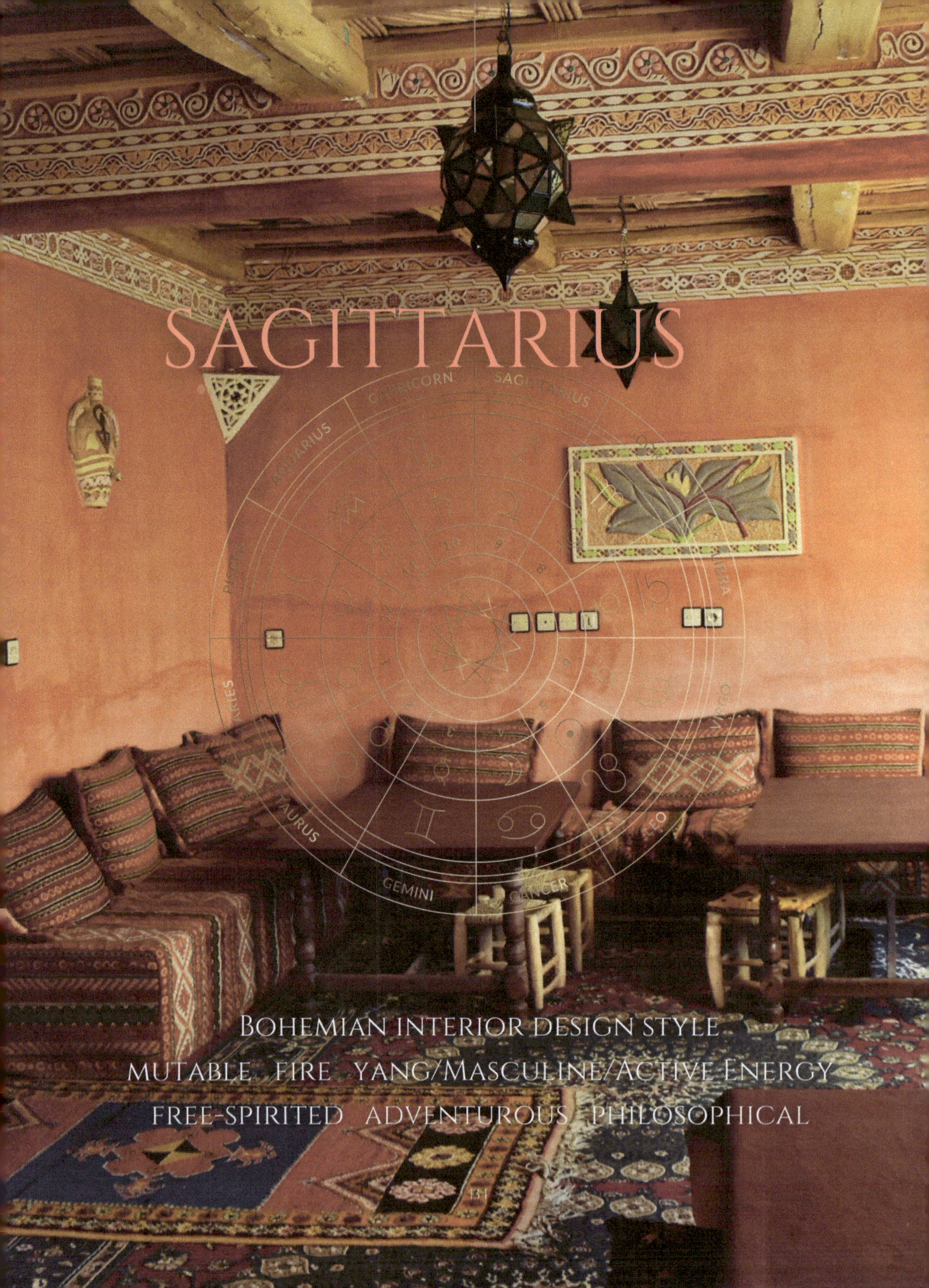

SAGITTARIUS

Bohemian interior design style
mutable fire yang/Masculine/Active Energy
free-spirited adventurous philosophical

CHAPTER 9
SAGITTARIUS

A Sagittarius is the eternal optimist and the explorer all rolled into one. They are the cosmic adventurers of the zodiac, armed with a laugh and an insatiable curiosity. Life with a Sagittarius is a rollercoaster, where every twist and turn is met with fun, curiosity, and an unquenchable thirst for the next great escape. These comedians are armed with a joke for every occasion and a burst of infectious and therapeutic laughter.

These free-spirited wanderers seek the next thrill or the universe's hidden treasures and knowledge. Sagittarius's approach to life is like a never-ending quest for the whirlwind of experiences and spiritual wisdom. The boundless curiosity of a Sagittarius mirrors the pursuit of knowledge as an art form. Constant enlightenment seekers traverse the cosmos to seek profound ideas and grand revelations. The inimitable optimism of a Sagittarius transcends conventional boundaries and echoes their infectious optimism.

Honesty is their cosmic superpower. They navigate the intricate dance of social niceties with the grace of a Jupitarian centaur in a china shop.
Need an unfiltered opinion? Consult your Sagittarius friend.
Commitment, however, is a word they consider as elusive as a shooting star.
The thought of being tethered to routine sends shivers down their spine. If you plan to pin down a Sagittarius, remember that the key is spontaneity.
Sagittarius are cosmic jesters, navigating the celestial expanse with universal wisdom, an irrepressible spirit and infectious laughter aimed at
The heart of life's grand tapestry.

CHAPTER 9
SAGITTARIUS

PERSONALITY/ELEMENTS/ RULING PLANET

Sagittarius is the mutable fire sign, the zodiac's last fire sign. Sagittarians are spirited with a dynamic force, enthusiasm, and a relentless thirst for adventure. These cosmic explorers of the zodiac constantly seek new horizons and thrilling experiences. Their insatiable curiosity and love for adventure drive them to embark on journeys that expand their understanding of the physical and spiritual world.

Born between November 22 and December 21, Sagittarius's ruling planet, Jupiter, is our solar system's largest planet. This cosmic alliance explains the Sagittarian's expansive nature, making them the perpetual seekers of wisdom, truth, and the boundless wonders of the universe. Sagittarians are born educators who desire to share their knowledge and experiences. They make excellent mentors, inspiring others to think beyond conventional boundaries and encouraging a lifelong love of higher learning.

Sagittarius's season transitions fall into winter on the day of the winter solstice in the Northern Hemisphere and spring into summer in the Southern Hemisphere on December 21 every year. This mutable energy provides a personality trait that can adapt and adjust to others, but is far from a pushover. Sagittarius's mutable quality of impatience thrives on change and variety, often seeking novel experiences to satiate their need for excitement.

CHAPTER 9
SAGITTARIUS

They are big dreamers, always aiming high, chasing the next big thing, not afraid of taking significant risks to reach their goals and dreams, and always very optimistic about the future due to the Jupiterian larger-than-life influence. Their positivity and optimism are contagious, and they possess an innate ability to see the silver lining even in the stormiest clouds.

Sagittarius signifies the ninth house of education, religion, spirituality, beliefs, and long-distance travel in the natural zodiac wheel, reflecting the philosophical inclination that marks Sagittarius's intellectual prowess.

They have a deep and expansive mind, exploring spirituality, philosophy, and higher knowledge. They embrace challenges as opportunities to expand their horizons and better understand themselves and their world.

Sagittarians are loyal people who are always there for their loved ones. They are very good at hiding their pain or hurt, can be distant, and need alone time; however, they do not hold grudges. They are independent and thrive on having freedom. They cannot be controlled and can't stay in one place too long. They resent drama, dislike others telling them what to do, and dislike people with hostile personalities. Sagittarians are known for their candidness and honesty.

They speak their mind with a refreshing bluntness, aligning with their commitment to authenticity, often forgetting the nuances of diplomacy. They can not stand people who are self-centred, selfish, deceitful or dishonest.

CHAPTER 9
SAGITTARIUS

This Yang/Masculine (non-gender specific) fire sign is highly active, energetic and passionate. Gifted with the art of persuasion, Sagittarians are charismatic communicators. Their warmth and friendliness make them natural conversationalists, great at engaging people from all walks of life. Sagittarius is a fun-loving, easy-going, flamboyant person who loves indulging and being surrounded by beautiful things. Their charm and sense of humour are captivating. Relationships serve as profound avenues for personal growth for Sagittarians. Interactions with diverse individuals allow them to expand their perspectives, deepen their understanding of emotions, and Navigate the complexities of human connections.

Sagittarians are exceptionally generous souls with open hearts. They enjoy sharing their experiences, knowledge, and resources with others. Their benevolence extends beyond material gifts, encompassing a willingness to offer guidance and support to those in need. The expansive nature of Sagittarius extends to a profound appreciation for cultural diversity. They are drawn to different customs, traditions, and perspectives, enjoying immersing themselves in the richness of global experiences. A sense of justice and fairness drives the Jupiterian nature of Sagittarians, who are inclined towards charitable endeavours, humanitarian causes, or social justice movements, using their passion and energy to contribute positively to society.

CHAPTER 9
SAGITTARIUS

INTERIOR DESIGN STYLE

Designing an interior space for a Sagittarius involves capturing their free-spirited, adventurous nature, love for exploration, and vibrant energy. They love parties, having fun, entertaining, and socializing with friends and family. Bright and cheerful walls, colourful decor, and artwork showcase this.
Fire signs' creative and adventurous nature.

Due to this sign's fun-loving and easy-going nature, a Sagittarian space is a relatively easy task to design, decorate, or furnish. Bohemian or Boho Interior Design Style embraces a mix of patterns, textures, and vibrant colours, allowing for a dynamic and personalized space that aligns with Sagittarius's appreciation for cultural diversity, their love for travel and exploration, creating an intriguing and visually stimulating environment.

Bohemian and Rustic Boho styles blend ethic or tribal-inspired pieces and motifs, and the love for nature with a free-spirited, nonconformist design vibe. It is a flamboyant yet cozy and inviting style that complements Sagittarius's fun-loving, adventurous and down-to-earth qualities and allows Sagittarians express their dynamic personality with gusto.
Embraces the worldly, larger-than-life Jupiterian philosophy and the "More is more, Sagittarius generosity, creating a stimulating and energetic environment.

CHAPTER 9
SAGITTARIUS

Infuse the space with ethnic or tribal furnishings and decor items inspired by different cultures. Sagittarians are keenly interested in worldwide explorations. Incorporate pieces like tribal prints, ethnic textiles, or artifacts collected from various regions to reflect Sagittarius's worldly, larger-than-life personality. Decorate walls with travel-inspired artwork, such as travel posters or photographs from their favourite destinations, reflecting their love for exploration and adding a personalized touch to the space.

Select versatile and flexible furniture that adapts to different uses. Sagittarians appreciate functionality and often prefer furniture that serves multiple purposes. Consider modular or foldable pieces that allow for easy rearrangement. A sofa with removable and washable covers or a convertible coffee table can accommodate their dynamic lifestyle. Prioritize comfortable seating with plush cushions and cozy throws. A mix of textures, such as faux fur, leather and natural fabrics, adds depth to the decor.

Carry the adventurous theme into the bedroom with bedding and decor that evoke affection and a sense of escape. Consider provocative, sensual patterns like animal or tribal prints to ignite passion and excitement. A canopy bed with gauzy curtains can evoke a sense of escape and stimulate their love and sexual energy. Hang personalized art or photographs above the bed, showcasing favourite travel destinations or dreamy landscapes.

CHAPTER 9
SAGITTARIUS

Sagittarius is a passionate fire sign and loves sensual and intriguing interiors. Select flexible lighting options to create different moods in the space. Consider adjustable pendant fixtures, track lighting, floor lamps, or string lights for various activities, from reading to entertaining guests. Design cozy reading nooks or lounging areas with comfortable seating and a selection of travel books or philosophical literature. Sagittarians enjoy immersing themselves in thought-provoking reads. Embrace natural light using sheer curtains or light-filtering blinds to maintain a bright and airy atmosphere during the day. Incorporate decor elements that evoke a sense of adventure, such as items like vintage suitcases, a world map as a mural, artistic interpretations of famous landmarks, or even a display of outdoor gear to showcase their adventurous spirit. Use stylish storage solutions or even vintage suitcases as decorative elements. Decorate with inspiring quotes or artwork that resonates with Sagittarius's philosophical nature, like motivational sayings, quotes from famous explorers, or artwork that reflects their love for the pursuit of knowledge and wisdom. Create curated displays of travel souvenirs, such as seashells, trinkets, or cultural artifacts, on open shelves or display cabinets.

The key to designing a Bohemian Interior Design style is to create an open-flow space and merge that echoes Sagittarius's freedom-loving, passionate and fiery nature, emulating their cosmopolitan mind and love for exploration.

CHAPTER 9
SAGITTARIUS

COLOURS

Sagittarius, a fire sign known for its dynamic and adventurous personality, is the best colour for interior design. The vibrant, fiery hues representing passion match the larger-than-life, optimistic, philosophical, and Spiritual nature of the last fire sign of the zodiac.

Deep, intense reds, sophisticated purples and aubergines are regal colours, implying the fire element that aligns with Sagittarius's expansive and luxurious Jupitarian nature. Consider using these warm, exaggerated hues for bedrooms and intimate retreat corners to create a personal sanctuary.

Applying these sophisticated, regal tones suggests class and sensuality and excites the room.

Golden yellows and bold oranges add an optimistic, lively, energetic vibe to the interior, representing creativity, joy, and positivity. Apply these colours throughout home offices by selecting antique-painted writing desks and vibrant modern office chairs, or even use them as a feature wall to boost creativity and productivity in the workspace. Textiles and ceramics of earth tones, like caramel and terracotta, resonate with Sagittarius's connection to the outdoors and nature to create a warm, cozy, grounded interior.

Sharp whites, warm grey, and the deeper tones of charcoal signify the air element that creates an elegant, balanced contrast in the interior space and energetically complements Sagittarius's fire element and intellectual mind.

CHAPTER 9
SAGITTARIUS

FENG SHUI

Designing the interior for Sagittarius's adventurous, worldly and philosophical spirit, associated with the dynamic fire sign, is exciting. And active Yang/Masculine (non-gender specific) energy. In Feng Shui, the Bagua map divides space into nine areas, each corresponding to different aspects of life. For Sagittarius, the last fire sign on the zodiac wheel, and an active Yang/Masculine (non-gender specific) energy correlates to the Fame and Reputation section on the Bagua Map, located on the south portion of the home, which embodies the fire element in traditional Feng Shui.

Intense, warm colours like red, orange, and yellow imply the fire element, stimulating Sagittarius' vibrant, fiery energy. Consider using these colours as accent walls, decor elements, or furniture upholstery. Enhance this area with a focal point like a red statement piece, a gallery wall of achievements, or a well-lit display to boost recognition and success energies. Place candles or fire-themed lighting fixtures strategically in the fame and reputation area to ignite or boost the fire element.
Avoid heavy or dark artwork that may dampen the vibrant energy associated with Sagittarius. Choose artwork and decor reflecting Sagittarius's curious mind, such as travel-themed pieces or items symbolizing exploration and growth. Steer clear of heavy or dark artwork that may dampen the vibrant energy.

CHAPTER 9
SAGITTARIUS

Feng Shui seeks to balance the energies of Yin/Feminine (passive) and Yang/Masculine (active). As a fire sign, Sagittarius represents the active, Yang/Masculine (non-gender specific) energy associated with the Sun.

Open up and energize the room by maximizing natural sunlight and implementing sheer curtains or blinds for window treatments that allow daylight to filter in and create an airy and expansive atmosphere while maintaining privacy.

Strategically placed mirrors reflect natural light and visually extend the room, making the space feel larger and brighter. Choose artwork and decor that resonate with Sagittarius' adventurous and optimistic nature: inspirational quotes, travel-themed artwork, or pieces representing exploration and growth.

Incorporate wooden decor to provide a harmonious balance, as the wood element feeds the fire element of the Five Elements cycle in traditional Feng Shui.

Introduce tall, upward-growing plants to symbolize the wood element, growth and expansion. Greenery resembles the natural world and promotes health, making the space feel homey and inviting.

CHAPTER 9
SAGITTARIUS

Design a secluded area devoted to personal, spiritual and emotional growth. Incorporate well-lit, organized and accessible bookshelves with open and closed storage spaces to accommodate and display books, magazines, or educational materials to satisfy Sagittarius's intellectual thirst for curiosity. Their unique sanctuary must be bright and sunny to ignite creativity and the passion for learning.

Choose artwork depicting landscapes, maps, or inspirational quotes related to travel and adventure that reflect the Sagittarius's excitement and thrill-loving nature. Include artwork with vibrant, uplifting themes and colours to resonate with Sagittarius' optimism. Opt for lighter topics as inspiration and brighter colour artwork to align with the light and fiery energy associated with Sagittarius. Display souvenirs from travels prominently to celebrate Sagittarius' love for exploration. Create a dedicated space, a personal Sanctuary to showcase achievements, diplomas, or certificates.

Incorporating these Feng Shui principles helps to create a personalized and balanced interior that aligns with Sagittarius's energetic qualities. Using the Bagua map, focusing on the fire element and the Fame and Reputation area of the home forms a space that supports Sagittarius's philosophical and spiritual nature and encourages a positive attitude toward recognition and success.

CAPRICORN

Farmhouse Interior Design Style
Cardinal Earth Yin/feminine/passive Energy
determent   practical   overachiever

CHAPTER 10
CAPRICORN

Capricorns approach life like seasoned CEOs. They have a strategic mindset, always thinking several steps ahead. Their ability to plan, organize, and execute with precision is unmatched. Saturn, the ruling planet of Capricorn, is like the stern principal overseeing the school of life. Capricorns adhere to a structured set of rules and principles and expect others to do the same.

These earth signs are natural mountain goat climbers in their careers and in every aspect of life. They set high standards for themselves and continuously strive for self-improvement. The metaphorical mountain they climb symbolizes their relentless pursuit of success, achievement, and, perhaps, a penthouse suite in the zodiac skyscraper, meticulously managing resources and planning for the future.

They know how to balance work and play and understand the importance of unwinding and enjoying life's festivities, but always with a calculated approach. Their Yin/Feminine is a mixed cosmic cocktail with precision, and they're the ones you can count on to be the designated drivers of the zodiac. Ensuring everyone gets home safely.

Capricorns are the celestial workaholics, responsible visionaries, and pragmatic dreamers of the zodiac. While their serious demeanour might make them seem like cosmic accountants, their disciplined and determined approach to life propels them to the zodiac's success ladder. Capricorns stand out like the overachieving ringleaders with a slightly uptight sense of responsibility; they are the ones you want in your celestial corner when things get tough.

CHAPTER 10
CAPRICORN

PERSONALITY/ELEMENTS/ RULING PLANET

Capricorn has a unique blend of Cardinal energy and an Earth element. Born between December 22nd and January 19th, Capricorns are ruled by the disciplined and structured planet Saturn. Signified by the symbol of the mountain goat, they embody qualities that define their approach to life, work, and relationships. Capricorn denotes the tenth sign and the 10th house of the zodiac wheel of public reputation, achievements, success, career, ambition, parental influences, authority, and public image.

Capricorn is the last earth sign and the last Cardinal sign of the four Cardinal signs, along with Aries, Cancer, and Libra. The Cardinal signs initiate each season, beginning a new astrological cycle. Capricorn heralds the start of winter, a season associated with hard work, perseverance, and preparation for the future. The Cardinal energy imbues Capricorns with a natural tendency to take charge, lead, and set ambitious goals. They are the cosmic architects, laying the groundwork for their and others' aspirations.

Their ruling planet, Saturn, with its leadership qualities, propels them to take charge and guide others toward collective success. They possess a unique leadership style, blending strategic thinking, pragmatic decision-making, and a calm and authoritative demeanour. They effortlessly assume the role of the captain, carefully planning each move to align with their long-term goals.

CHAPTER 10
CAPRICORN

As a cardinal earth sign, initiation and ambition course through the veins of Capricorns. Driven by the desire for success and recognition, they set lofty goals and work tirelessly to achieve them. Their determination and unwavering focus make them formidable competitors in any field. Their ability to think big and set challenging goals sets them apart. Capricorns aim for the stars and are willing to put in the Saturnian's hard work to turn their dreams into reality.

As an Earth sign, Capricorns share common traits with Taurus and Virgo. The Earth element lends practicality, stability, and a grounded approach to life. It serves as the solid foundation upon which Capricorns build their dreams. They understand the importance of rational, sensible steps to achieve their goals and avoid impulsive, offhand decision-making and unnecessary risks. While they may have ambitious dreams, Capricorns are firmly rooted in the present, carefully planning each step toward success.

With their astrological earth element and practical mindset, Capricorns excel in financial matters and understand the importance of saving, investing, and building a secure future, ensuring a stable economic foundation. Their earth element ensures they are stable, dependable individuals in personal relationships and professional settings. Others often turn to Capricorns for guidance and support to provide a steady and unwavering presence.

CHAPTER 10
CAPRICORN

Capricorns may present a reserved and harsh exterior, but beneath this facade lies a depth of emotions and thoughts. They carefully choose when and with whom to share their innermost feelings. They are reserved and private individuals, carefully guarding their emotions and personal lives. While they may not be the most expressive, their loyalty and dependability make them trusted confidants to those they choose to let into their inner circle.

Contrary to their serious exterior, Capricorns have a delightful sense of humour and a playful side. As a Saturnian stereotype, the stern Capricorn appreciates wit and cleverness, and their laughter can be infectious once they let their guard down. Their playfulness emerges in a trusted company, revealing a more lighthearted side that complements their otherwise levelheaded and pragmatic nature.

Capricorns often hold traditional values in high regard. They value hard work, loyalty, and commitment in professional and personal relationships. Tradition provides a framework that aligns with their sense of structure and order. These values provide a moral compass that guides their decisions and actions. The Capricorn personality shines as an unwavering commitment, loyalty, hard work, and virtue, embodying all aspects of life and leaving an indelible mark on the tapestry of the zodiac.

CHAPTER 10
CAPRICORN

INTERIOR DESIGN STYLE

Designing an interior space that aligns with the characteristics and preferences of a Capricorn, an astrological cardinal zodiac earth sign, involves incorporating elements that resonate with their practicality, ambition, and appreciation for the outdoors and nature.

Capricorns appreciate functionality as an earth sign and the traits of Saturn as the ruling planet of organized and orderly spaces. The grounded, earthy, Modern Farmhouse Interior Design Style achieves a sophisticated, timeless design that reflects Capricorn's nature. Select natural materials like wooden furniture, stone countertops, and leather upholstery to Enhance the Earth's elements further.

Opt for structured, well-built, practical furniture pieces with clean lines. A sturdy wooden desk for work or study is necessary for a Capricorn's space. Practical closed-in storage solutions maintain a visually clutter-free environment.

Create a comfortable yet ambitious atmosphere. Incorporate comfortable, relaxing seating and a dedicated workspace with a functional, practical layout conducive to focus and productivity. In their private home office, dedicate a wall or a stylish display unit to celebrate accomplishments and visually reinforce the Capricorn's commitment to success. Balance is vital to ensuring that the space caters to the Capricorn's need for a drive for success.

CHAPTER 10
CAPRICORN

Lighting is out to be practical and aesthetically pleasing. Choose lighting fixtures with clean lines, like lanterns or modern pendant chandeliers, to enhance the farmhouse design style. Selecting practical and aesthetically pleasing fixtures that provide ample artificial lighting for Workspaces and reading areas are crucial.

Consider incorporating lighting fixtures with exposed bulbs or metallic finishes to add a touch of sophistication and a polished look. Ensure adequate task lighting in workspaces and reading nooks, and add ambient lighting with floor or table lamps to create a comfortable and inviting atmosphere.

Integrate natural fibres like cotton, linen, and silk when selecting fabrics for a Capricorn home or office space. Carefully blend solids, tone-on-tone subtle geometrical patterns and organic leaf motifs into the decor and reflect Capricorn's structured personality and earth energy.
Solid neutral, classic, tailored drapery panels and Roman shades, combined with accent chairs upholstered with tone-on-tone stripes or geometrical patterns, dressed with decorative pillows of organic floral or leaf motives, create a
balanced and welcoming surroundings.

CHAPTER 10
CAPRICORN

Capricorn, as an earth sign, thrives on being surrounded by nature. Introduce plants and greenery to the space to connect with the Earth element. Fortunately, Capricorn is not afraid of work and extra effort, so plants that are high maintenance or require more care, like orchids or fiddle-leaf fig trees, align with Capricorn's determination and commitment. The presence of plants adds a natural touch and contributes to clean air, a healthier environment, and more vibrant surroundings. Select earth-tone decorative pots or planters to enhance the Earth element and bring a touch of nature indoors. Consider incorporating terrariums (glass containers like an aquarium for plants that look like a mini garden to include modern and visually appealing greenery.

Capricorns appreciate quality and longevity. Opt for timeless, well-made, durable furniture pieces and practical decor items. Avoid excessive ornamentation and prioritize a few well-chosen, high-quality items over an abundance of lesser-quality pieces. Choose materials and finishes that stand the test of time, ensuring the design remains relevant and appealing for years. Striking a balance between a structured, clean-lined interior design style and creating a practical, functional, and welcoming home for a Capricorn is vital to connect to the earth element to form a harmonious space that reflects this zodiac sign's unique personality traits and qualities.

CHAPTER 10
CAPRICORN

COLOURS

Decorating with colours for an astrological earth sign like Capricorn involves selecting a palette of earthy tones to create a grounding and welcoming atmosphere. Neutrals like warm whites, light sand, and taupe evoke a sense of elegance in a bright, airy environment.

Use neutral tones for larger pieces such as sofas, curtains, or bedding. Add deeper tones of brown or terracotta to generate contrast and excitement with subtle pops of colours.

Introduce shades of green, from soft sage to emerald green, representing growth and adding a peaceful touch to promote well-being.

Various shades of blues associated with the water element complement the earthy Capricorn home. Implying the Saturnian leadership, use darker shades of cobalt, royal, and navy blue as accent colours through accessories.

Decorative pieces in metallic finishes like copper, brass, or gold symbolize success and ambition, aligning with Capricorn's desire for leadership and achievement and adding elegance and glamour to the space.

The goal is to form a balanced, harmonious atmosphere reflecting Capricorn's practical nature. Experiment with these colour suggestions and decorating tips to tailor the design to the unique characteristics of the earth sign.

CHAPTER 10
CAPRICORN

FENG SHUI

Feng Shui is an ancient Chinese practice that involves arranging the space to create a harmonious flow of energy, known as Chi (Qi). The Bagua map is a vital tool in Feng Shui, representing various aspects of life and their corresponding areas in a space. The Bagua map divides space into nine regions, each corresponding to different aspects of life like Wealth, Fame, Love and Relationships, Family, Health, Children and Creativity, Knowledge, and Career. When decorating for a Capricorn, an earth sign, integrate Feng Shui principles to enhance their natural tendencies for stability, practicality, and ambition.

Capricorn, as an earth sign and a Yin/Feminine (non-gender specific) energy, emphasizes the earth element in the Bagua areas, which energetically aligns with the Farmhouse Interior Design Style. Use warm, earthy tones like browns, greens, and beige in decor and furnishings. Incorporate natural materials such as wood, stone, and ceramic to enhance the grounding energy in a Farmhouse or Traditional design and atmosphere.

Capricorns value education, knowledge and wisdom. Create a study or reading area to enhance the Knowledge, Wisdom, and Self-Improvement areas in the front left corner of the space. Use bookshelves, study areas, or artwork that represents wisdom and learning. Accent walls or furniture in dark green colours signify growth or a blend of dark navy, representing leadership and the water element, complementary to Capricorn's determination inherited from Saturn.

CHAPTER 10
CAPRICORN

Capricorns are ambitious and career-oriented people. The section that correlates and benefits Capricorn is typically at the front center of the space, in the Bagua Map's Life Path and Career square. Add symbols of success, such as awards or certifications, that signify ambition and use elements like dark wood, which resembles determination and long-lasting stability.

Position a desk or workspace in this area facing the door to welcome career prospects. Display symbols of success and achievements on the desk, keeping it clean and organized to reflect professionalism.

Activate the Prosperity, Wealth and Abundance area, usually located at the far left corner of the space, to attract financial growth. Use symbols of prosperity, like live money plants, eight lucky coins or fish bowls. With intention, water and wood elements in this area can enhance financial stability.

Decorate with items that symbolize prosperity, such as a wealth bowl or a symbol of abundance. Incorporate natural materials like wood, stone, and ceramic in furniture and decor, and use square or rectangular-shaped objects to strengthen the Earth's elements and stability.

Select gold, copper, and bronze metallic objects and finishes resembling prosperity and attracting abundance. Keep the area well-lit to promote positive energy flow and productivity.

CHAPTER 10
CAPRICORN

Capricorn appreciates family and unity. The Family & Community area on the Bagua Map is in the middle left section, essential for creating a stable family life. Use nurturing colours like greens and blues that support Capricorn's earth sign. Incorporate treasured family photos or symbols of unity to encourage and strengthen family bonds.

The Love and Relationships area is in the right-hand back corner of the Feng Shui Bagua Map space. Design the bedroom in a traditional, symmetrical manner, where each side is a mirrored image of the other, representing equality within the partnership. Use pairs of objects, like animal statues, a pair of candle holders, or artwork representing harmony, unity and partnership. Incorporate soft fabrics and romantic, fiery, passionate colours like wine and aubergine to enhance the fire element of this intimate area.

The center of the space signifies the Health & Well-being section of the Bagua Map. Keep this area clutter-free and well-lit. Use natural elements like earth-tone colours, comfort and protection, and blemish-free, live plants to promote physical, psychological and emotional well-being.

These essential Feng Shui tips consider the particular areas of the Bagua map to establish a harmonious and supportive environment tailored to the characteristics of a Capricorn individual.

AQUARIUS

CONTEMPORARY INTERIOR DESIGN STYLE
FIXED   AIR   YANG/MASCULINE/ACTIVE ENERGY
UNCONVENTIONAL   HUMANITARIAN   INDEPENDENT

CHAPTER 11
AQUARIUS

Welcome to the zodiac's avant-garde visionary – Aquarius, the celestial rebel who dances through the cosmos with an air of unpredictability and a heart fueled by innovation. Aquarians are the architects of the future, sketching out utopian blueprints in the margins of reality. Their dreams extend beyond the horizon, where conventional thinking gives way to the extraordinary.

Originality is their middle name, and Aquarians don't just march to the beat of a different drummer; they compose symphonies that resonate in the hearts of fellow cosmic wanderers. Social circles are their experimental playgrounds. Aquarians effortlessly blend with the eccentrics, the visionaries, and the rebels.

Love, for Aquarians, is an unconventional odyssey. Romantic gestures are cosmic adventures, and relationships are celestial unions. They seek a partner who understands that love is not confined to the gravitational pull of the ordinary. They bring a cosmic twist to romance. Forget flowers and candlelight dinners; they'll gift you a self-watering plant and a DIY picnic under the stars, flipping any detours on the way.

Aquarians don't follow trends. They are social chameleons, effortlessly blending with all the misfits, rebels, and free spirits at the intergalactic coffee shop. They are guided by an unwavering sense of justice that transcends earthly boundaries. They're the humanitarians of the zodiac, pushing for change with the conviction that a better world is not a distant galaxy but an achievable reality. Aquarians are the future philosophers, contemplating the mysteries of existence with a gaze fixed on the cosmic horizon.

CHAPTER 11
AQUARIUS

PERSONALITY/ELEMENTS/ RULING PLANET

Aquarius, the last air sign of the zodiac, born between January 20 and February 18, has fascinating and enigmatic individual characteristics and traits. Governed by Uranus as a modern ruler planet, signifying technology, rebellion, and unconventional, revolutionary, profound transformational qualities, and Saturn, as an ancient ruler, governs boundaries, governments, rulers, and responsibilities (some astrological sign, like Aquarius, has two ruler planet, depending on the astrological system), which explains the Water-Bearer's mystical healing and spiritual personality.

As a fixed sign, Aquarius exhibits steadfastness, determination, and resistance to change, unwavering in their pursuit once they set their sights on a goal or idea. Aquarians have a strong sense of social responsibility. They are innovators who can leave a lasting impact on the world. Their ideas, inventions, and contributions often endure, influencing the course of history and shaping the collective consciousness.

Astrologically speaking, the fixed Air sign combination allows Aquarians to balance stability with flexibility. While they maintain a steady course in their pursuits, they also possess the adaptability to navigate the changing winds of progress. They bring an unconventional twist to the idea of stability. Their fixed nature isn't necessarily rooted in tradition; it's grounded in pursuing their unique vision for the future in the ever-evolving realm of innovation.

CHAPTER 11
AQUARIUS

Aquarius embodies the eleventh house of the astrological zodiac wheel, signifying friendship, alliances, hopes and dreams; social media and the internet exhibit this air sign's social butterfly nature. They typically enjoy meeting new people and building long-term relationships, and are loyal to their friends. Aquarians are known for their fiercely independent and unconventional thinking. Their minds are like laboratories, constantly experimenting with novel concepts and pushing the boundaries of what's possible. They challenge authority and question established norms, social reform, and Challenging outdated systems.

Aquarians can show a certain level of emotional detachment. Their air sign nature makes them objective and rational thinkers capable of being emotionally detached and objectively analyzing situations. They value mental connections and friendships as much as romantic bonds.
In relationships, Aquarians are forward-looking and appreciate a companion who respects their need for independence. They value deep connections based on shared interests and intellectual compatibility. Aquarians are emotionally selective, which explains their sometimes cold and rigid exterior and demeanour. Emotional intimacy may take time to develop as they Prioritize mental connections in relationships.

CHAPTER 11
AQUARIUS

Forward-thinking visionaries by nature, Aquarians have a deep-seated desire to contribute to the betterment of humanity; often, they are ahead of their time. They are natural humanitarians, driven by a sense of justice and a passion for societal progress.

Aquarians envision a world beyond the current status quo and are advocates of social justice. Their innate sense of fairness drives them to fight for equality, and they are often vocal about issues related to civil rights.

Inclusivity and societal harmony.

They enjoy engaging in thought-provoking conversations, contemplating abstract concepts, and exploring the mysteries of the universe. As fixed Air signs, they are analytical and approach problem-solving objectively. Emotions rarely cloud their judgment. Instead, they use logical reasoning and a detached perspective to navigate challenges.

Aquarius combines intellectual brilliance with a commitment to societal progress. Governed by the element of air, they thrive on innovation and eccentricity. From their rebellious spirit to their visionary pursuits, Aquarians leave an indelible mark on the world as pioneers of progress and advocates for a more enlightened tomorrow.

CHAPTER 11
AQUARIUS

INTERIOR DESIGN STYLE

Try creating a space with a modern or contemporary interior design style for the visionary Aquarius. These design styles correlate with their innovative, revolutionary, and cutting-edge astrological personality traits. Incorporate spacious, undivided design layouts with large windows, wall-to-wall patio doors, and openings to allow natural light to flow and the home to feel bright. Avoid clutter and heavy furnishings to enhance the expanded feel of the space.

Aquarians are fascinated by innovation and futuristic ideas. Select furniture with avant-garde, clean lines, sleek finishes, and contemporary aesthetics. Opt for pieces that have a pioneering appeal, such as minimalist sofas, acrylic chairs, or tables with clean geometric shapes and metallic finishes like chrome or silver to add a touch to reflect Aquarius's futuristic and visionary personality. Aquarians appreciate uniqueness and individuality. Consider modern furnishings with open seating arrangements and comfortable contemporary lounge furniture with conversational seating arrangements to foster family and social engagement. Incorporate one-of-a-kind artworks or design elements that reflect this intellectual Air sign's distinct, unconventional personality. Create a secluded reading nook that provides Aquarius with a private space for reading or studying intellectual interests. Include a comfortable chair, a stylish bookshelf, and efficient, layered lighting appropriate for the function.

CHAPTER 11
AQUARIUS

Aquarians appreciate carefully designed, thoughtful spaces within their home that stimulate their mind and intellectual pursuits. Given the association with technology, Aquarius integrates futuristic gadgets and Modern technological advancements in design.

Consider incorporating smart, high-tech home devices, interactive art installations, or a media room with the latest entertainment technology integrated seamlessly into the design. Smart home devices, voice-controlled assistants, interactive elements, and tech-savvy homes or offices equipped with the latest gadgets are the perfect additions for an Aquarian. Lighting is crucial in interior design, setting the ambiance for the air sign, Aquarius, as they thrive in a bright, airy environment. Select modern, highbrowed statement lighting fixtures with a futuristic vibe, illuminating the space and serving as artistic focal points.

Designing the space with contemporary, peculiar fixtures forms an extraordinary layer of design reflecting Aquarius's Uranus-influenced unconventional trait. One-of-a-kind, artistic, sculptured statement pendant lights with unique and bold black, white or silver metallic designs capture attention and reflect an out-of-the-ordinary personality.

CHAPTER 11
AQUARIUS

An eco-conscious approach to design aligns with Aquarius's humanitarian values. Select sustainable materials for flooring and interior finishes, energy-efficient lighting, and environmentally friendly furnishings. Decorate with trendy, innovative indoor live walls made of plants to bring a touch of nature into the space.

Aquarians appreciate intellectually stimulating art and decor items. Display items such as travel souvenirs, unique collections, or art pieces that resonate with their beliefs and values and reflect the Aquarian individuality. Incorporating thought-provoking, interactive, contemporary art that conveys intellectual depth can create a visually engaging environment.

Displaying travel souvenirs, tech gadgets, or avant-garde collectibles and incorporating meaningful elements into the decor adds a personalized and authentic touch to the space.

These suggestions are general guidelines, and personal preferences play a significant role in creating a Modern Interior Design style and an individualized space for the eccentric Aquarius. Ultimately, the goal is to make a unique home or office space that feels authentic and inspiring and resonates. This zodiac air sign resembles intellectual brilliance and commitment to Societal progress of the zodiac sign Aquarius.

CHAPTER 11
AQUARIUS

COLOURS

Decorating for an air sign like Aquarius with a colour palette of white, grey, charcoal, and black signifies the air element and supports the Modern or Contemporary Interior Design Style. White represents clarity, openness, and a blank canvas for innovative ideas conducive to Aquarius. Incorporate crisp white as the dominant colour for walls or larger surfaces to create a calm atmosphere, allowing other colours and design elements to stand out.

A modern or contemporary design style typically involves a monochromatic colour scheme within the space. Blend cool, light greys with tone-on-tone geometrical patterns and apply draperies, curtains, sheers, and upholstery for sofas, chairs, or cushions to form contrast and classy, elegant surroundings. Dark or charcoal gray adds depth to the space while maintaining a sense of neutrality. Use charcoal gray for artwork, larger furniture pieces, accent walls, or rugs and flooring as a grounding element. Use black for small decor items to limit mental fatigue and avoid visually sinking the room.
Metallic tones like silver and chrome reflect Aquarius's association with innovation and modern technology. Use faux fur, knit, or woven tactile textures to create a style that aligns with Aquarius's appreciation for artistic pursuits.
Add a pop of colour to reflect individual tastes,
a personal flair inspired by Aquarius's offbeat nature.

CHAPTER 11
AQUARIUS

FENG SHUI

Elements play a significant role in Feng Shui and Astrology, but there are differences in how these systems categorize and associate elements. Decorating with Feng Shui and the Bagua map for an Aquarius, a fixed air sign, involves creating a harmonious and balanced space that supports their independent personalities. The Bagua Map is an essential tool in Feng Shui. It is divided into nine areas, each corresponding to different aspects of life.

Feng Shui defines five elements in nature: Fire, Earth, Metal, Water, and Wood, to balance the energy (Chi or Qi) in space. In Feng Shui, the metal element denotes clarity, precision, structure, and metal objects and colours such as white, grey, and metallic tones. The air element in astrology and the metal element in Feng Shui share associations with intellectual pursuits and clarity of thought. They signify a focus on mental activities, communication, and precision. When incorporating Feng Shui principles into a space for an air sign like Aquarius, consider enhancing.
The metal area is associated with the Bagua Map.
Aquarius aligns with the characteristics of this air sign's Yang/Masculine (non-gender specific) active energy: angular furniture pieces and structured lines resembling stability relating to the Fixed trait of Aquarius. Metal represents Yang's energy and precision, aligning with Aquarius's analytical mindset.

CHAPTER 11
AQUARIUS

Aquarius is associated with the Helpful People, Travel & Future area in the front-right section of the Bagua map. This area influences innovation, networking, and supportive connections. Blend colours associated with the Future/Helpful People, the North/West section, such as metallic colours like silver and chrome, to attract auspicious business and personal connections. Aquarius is an air sign, and metal is the corresponding element. Incorporate metal decor items like metallic frames, sculptures, or small accent furniture.

Create a dedicated study or workspace to support Aquarius's intellectual pursuits. Place a desk or work area in the Knowledge/Wisdom/Self-Improvement area of the Bagua map of the front left corner. Apply intense, fiery colours to enhance concentration and wisdom. Aquarians are visionaries. Display vision boards or inspirational quotes in the Life Path/Career area (front-center) to symbolize their forward-thinking nature. Incorporate images that represent their aspirations and goals.

Ensure a balance of Yin and Yang energies. Use a mix of soft textures, like rugs and cushions, to introduce Yin qualities while incorporating angular and structured furniture for Yang energy. Use a blend of silky textures, like rugs and pillows, to introduce Yin qualities while incorporating angular and structured furniture for Yang energy.

CHAPTER 11
AQUARIUS

Aquarians thrive in uncluttered environments. Keep spaces organized and clutter-free. Use storage closed-in or hidden solutions to maintain a clean and streamlined appearance, allowing energy to flow freely throughout the room. The Bagua map incorporates wood elements and plants to connect with the Wood area. Wood elements like plants or vertical live walls represent growth and vitality, supporting Aquarius's desire for progress and positive change. Display personalized items and art that resonate with Aquarius's interests and values, including artwork related to technology, innovation, or humanitarian causes. Incorporate silver-coloured metallic elements in decor accents or fixtures like lamps or drawer pulls.
These tones add a sleek and futuristic touch to the overall design. Aquarians enjoy personal partnership and appreciate unconventional expressions of love and romance. Their rigid nature sometimes feels detached. Use warm colours and welcoming, comfortable seating arrangements in Bagua map's Love/Relationships section (back-right corner) to Encourage social interactions and intimate connections.
Feng Shui is about creating a balanced and harmonious environment that supports the individual's well-being. Adapt these principles to suit personal preferences and the specific characteristics of the Aquarian individual for a more personalized and practical approach to decorating.

PISCES

Transitional Interior design Style
mutable   water   Yin/feminine/passive Energy
empathetic   spiritual   imaginative

CHAPTER 12
PISCES

Pisces, the dreamers of the zodiac, where reality and fantasy engage, and you've landed in the whimsical realm of a Piscean mind. Reality is just a backdrop for their vivid imagination. Symbolized by two fish swimming in opposite directions, Pisceans navigate life like synchronized swimmers in a chaotic ballet.

Pisces have more emotional layers; they can switch from tearful empathy to contagious laughter. Pisces love to keep an air of mystery. Pisceans experience emotions like they're painting with a watercolour palette – soft washes of sensitivity and bold strokes of passion.

If you think a Pisces is psychic, you're probably onto something. Their intuition is so sharp that it's practically a sixth sense. They might not predict the lottery numbers, but they'll sense your emotional storm from miles away.

Pisces individuals are the DIY philosophers of the zodiac. They've contemplated the meaning of life. If you feel down, they'll wrap you in a blanket of empathy, offer you metaphorical hot cocoa, and It strangely makes you feel understood.

Creativity flows through Pisceans like water through a river. They're poets, artists, and musicians who can turn a mundane trip to the grocery store into a symphony of inspiration in the grand tapestry of the zodiac, Pisces nation, the melody of empathy, and a touch of mystical enchantment.

CHAPTER 12
PISCES

PERSONALITY/ELEMENTS/ RULING PLANET

Pisces, the mutable water sign, is the ethereal dreamer of the zodiac, embodying Yin/Feminine (non-gender specific) passive energy, which is receptive, intuitive, and nurturing. Pisces individuals have a penchant for daydreaming and escaping into their fantastical worlds. Reality often feels like a mere backdrop to their rich inner life. This dreamy quality can make them enchanting and elusive as they navigate between the tangible and the surreal.

Piscean people are born between February 19 and March 20, shifting from winter to spring in the Northern Hemisphere and from Fall into Winter in the Southern Hemisphere, transitioning into the spring equinox on the Northern Hemisphere and fall equinox on the Southern Hemisphere on March 21 every year. Pisces is the twelfth sign, the last sign of the zodiac, and it represents the twelfth house on the Astrological wheel, signifying.
Spirituality, mystery, solitude, and self-sabotage in astrology.
As a mutable water sign, Pisces epitomizes the Yin/Feminine energy with its profound emotional nature. They are highly attuned to their feelings and possess an oceanic depth of emotions. Pisceans are natural empaths and absorb the feelings of those around them, making them exceptionally attuned to the needs and feelings of others. Pisces' zodiac symbol is two fish swimming in opposite directions, signifying its mutable and adaptive nature.

CHAPTER 12
PISCES

In traditional Astrology, Pisces' ruling planets are Jupiter and Neptune in modern Astrology. Each planet uniquely influences the personality traits and characteristics of the zodiac sign Pisces.

Jupiter is the planet of philosophy, spirituality, expansion, growth, and optimism. When associated with Pisces, it amplifies the compassionate, expansive, and generous nature, often open-mindedness and acceptance of diverse beliefs and cultures. They are naturally curious about the world and willing to explore different ideologies, making them adaptable and flexible. Jupiter is often associated with luck and positive outcomes. Pisceans with a strong Jupiter influence may experience serendipitous events or find themselves in fortunate situations.

Neptune is the planet of dreams, illusions, and imagination. As the modern ruler of Pisces, Neptune enhances the dreamy and otherworldly spiritual qualities of the natural, compassionate empath. Pisceans influenced by Neptune often have a rich inner life and a heightened sensitivity to the unseen realms, making them warm-hearted healers and sympathetic listeners. They feel a profound connection to the collective human experience, exploring mystical experiences of their spiritual journey. On the flip side, Neptune's influence can contribute to a tendency for escapism and seeing situations through rose-coloured glasses.

CHAPTER 12
PISCES

Pisces' adaptable, flexible, dreamy, and idealistic quality extends to their creativity, where they thrive in fluid and ever-changing artistic expressions. Through visual arts, music, or writing, Pisceans are natural visionaries with a boundless imagination. Neptune fosters artistic and creative expression in Pisceans and excels in visual arts, music, dance, or other forms of creative communication. Neptune's psychic and intuitive trait adds a touch of magic and inspiration to their artistic endeavours.

The ruling planets of Pisces, Jupiter and Neptune, the two largest gaseous planets in our solar system, contribute to Pisces' multifaceted and nuanced personality traits. Jupiter brings optimism, expansiveness, and an intellectual, philosophical outlook, while Neptune adds dreaminess, empathy, and a connection to the mystical and imaginative spiritual realms.

These planetary influences make Pisces a sign rich in creativity, compassion, and spiritual awareness. Their connection to the divine and open-minded exploration of metaphysical realms are vital aspects of their spiritual journey. Pisces is a tender soul embodying spirituality, mysticism and the receptive and nurturing qualities of the Yin/Feminine energy, navigating the seas of emotions deeply with colossal spiritual wisdom as the last zodiac sign in Astrology.

CHAPTER 12
PISCES

INTERIOR DESIGN STYLE

Forming a mood and atmosphere resembling water is essential when designing a Piscean home. The Transitional Interior Design Style, blending traditional and contemporary elements, aligns well with the last mutable water sign of the zodiac. With a creative mind, Pisceans appreciate change and design zones that can easily transition between different purposes. Integrate a mix of traditional and contemporary furniture pieces that mirror Pisces' creative, open-minded and adaptive nature. Consider pairing a modern sofa with accent chairs with soft lines and gentle curves.
The fluidity in design reflects Pisces's mutable and creative side, building a sense of ease and flow within the space.

Pisces may prioritize the needs of others over their own. They can make themselves self-sacrificial, sometimes to the point of neglecting their well-being, leading them to escapist tendencies or even addictive behaviours. Design spaces that adapt to various activities, like a meditation room, a cozy reading nook or an artistic workspace. Invest in multifunctional furniture that serves different purposes, like a sectional sofa with ottomans, allowing for a living space that can adapt to various activities. With a sensitive personality, Pisces appreciates a private sanctuary in their home that provides a cozy and safe environment for self-reflection and personal growth.

CHAPTER 12
PISCES

Create corners dedicated to artistic pursuits. Include an easel, art supplies, or a crafting table where Pisces can engage in creative projects that align with their artistic inclinations. Decorate the walls with inspirational quotes or affirmations that resonate with Pisces's spiritual side. Add shelves filled with books and literature of love, fantasy, poetry, spiritual, esoteric and mystical in nature. Designate spaces for quiet reflection, like placing a comfortable chair by a window, a meditation corner, or a cozy fireplace spot.

Introduce reflective surfaces, such as silver accents, mirrors, glass, or metallic accents, to enhance the dreamy and introspective qualities associated with Pisces. Mirrors also contribute to the water element, symbolizing fluidity and reflection. Consider pieces with water motifs, abstract paintings, or ethereal landscapes. Showcase personal and sentimental items like handmade crafts, travel souvenirs, or family heirlooms. Display artwork that combines traditional and contemporary elements that reflect Pisces' artistic sensibilities. Select soft and tranquil colours inspired by the ocean, such as gentle blues, aquas, and seafoam blues, to cast a calming, serene atmosphere that resonates with Pisces' water element. Incorporate blue accent walls, a trendy epoxy tabletop with a flowy water-like pattern, painted furniture, nautical accessories, or textiles with gentle blue tones to create a mystical yet welcoming home.

CHAPTER 12
PISCES

Incorporate soft textures and comfortable fabrics in upholstery and furnishings. Pisces appreciates cozy and nurturing environments. Plush cushions, throw blankets, and textured rugs add a touch of comfort and warmth. The more relaxed, the better. Soft, tactile textures like faux fur and knitted fabrics enhance the sensory experience and create a cozy atmosphere. Use flowing fabrics and sheer curtains to evoke a sense of movement and fluidity.

Bring the outdoors inside with abundant indoor plants, botanical patterns and wood fishes. Pisceans have a profound connection to nature, and greenery can promote a sense of tranquillity. Adding water features like fountains or a The fish tank represents the water element and attracts an abundance.

Install flexible lighting solutions with a mix of traditional and modern fixtures. Adjustable floor lamps, pendant lights, or sconces provide adaptable lighting, allowing Pisceans to create different atmospheres based on their mood or activity. Enhance the sensory emotions with scented candles or essential oil diffusers for a spiritual experience that Piscean people appreciate.
The Transitional Interior Design allows for a seamless blending of styles, making it ideal for Pisces. Blending traditional and contemporary elements is a practical design choice for Pisces' mutable and ever-changing nature.

CHAPTER 12
PISCES

COLOURS

Selecting colour palettes, textures and tones resembling the water element that resonates with deep emotions and a creative, whimsical, and imaginative spirit enhances the Piscean home, providing a soothing and nurturing atmosphere.
Consider hues like aqua, seafoam, and powder blue that evoke serenity. Infusing mystical indigo blue adds a touch of magic, mystery, and depth to the room, enhancing romantic connection and contributing to the dreamy and introspective qualities associated with Pisces.

Accent colours of mint, soft sage, mossy, apple greens and earth tones add a grounding earth element that is naturally aligned with this water sign, Pisces, bringing freshness and tranquillity to the space. Soft neutrals like off-whites and creams provide a gentle backdrop and form a harmonious canvas that maintains a balanced and airy feel.

Silver-cloured metallic decor accents like vases, picture frames, or metallic-finish furniture capture the reflective qualities of water
and add elegance and an enchanting atmosphere to the home.
These colours resonate with Pisces's dreamy and emotionally rich nature. The key is to balance the mystical elements that capture this water sign's essence and to create a calm and grounding atmosphere within their home.

CHAPTER 12
PISCES

FENG SHUI

Feng Shui, the ancient Chinese art of arranging surroundings to promote harmony and balance, offers a powerful tool, the Bagua Map, for creating a tranquil and positive living space. The connection between Pisces as a water sign in astrology and the Bagua Map lies in understanding the elemental association of each sign and its corresponding areas in the Bagua. In Feng Shui, the Bagua Map is divided into nine regions, each linked to a specific aspect of life and associated with one of the five elements—Wood, Fire, Earth, Metal, and Water. As a water sign, Pisces correlates with the water element.

In the Bagua Map, the Water element is primarily associated with the north direction, and the Bagua's north area is considered the Water element's natural domain. However, it's important to note that the Bagua Map is flexible, and the elemental associations can vary based on different schools of Feng Shui.

Pisces adore enhancing their living space following their astrological sign; focusing on the north area of the Bagua Map is a good starting point. This area corresponds to Bagua's Life Path and Career aspect, which can be particularly significant for Pisces seeking to navigate their path with fluidity and intuition. Pisces, the twelfth sign of the zodiac, is known for its dreamy, compassionate, artistic, and spiritual nature.

CHAPTER 12
PISCES

In Feng Shui, the concept of Yin and Yang is fundamental. Yin represents the passive, receptive, and feminine (non-gender specific) energy, while Yang embodies the active, dynamic, and masculine (non-gender specific) energy. The water element in Feng Shui is associated with Yin energy, and for Pisces, A water sign, this connection can be particularly significant.

Decorating with Yin energy, as a water element for Pisces, involves creating a space reflects Yin and water's soothing, nurturing, and introspective qualities.

Incorporate soft and plush textures in furnishings, such as comfortable rugs, cushions, and throws that add a tactile dimension to the space, enhancing the Yin energy and promoting a cozy and nurturing environment. Opt for decor items with flowing, curved shapes to mimic water's gentle, meandering nature to create a harmonious and Yin-inspired atmosphere.

For Pisceans, enhancing the southeast area of the home can boost prosperity and abundance. Use soothing water elements like a small fountain or artwork featuring water scenes to invite positive energy flow.

Pisces' desire for recognition and appreciation focuses on the south-center area of the home of Fame and Reputation. Incorporate artwork or symbol recognition that reflects their artistic talents and showcases achievements.

CHAPTER 12
PISCES

Pisces thrives on deep emotional connections, focusing on the southwest area of Relationships, Love and Marriage. Use romantic décor and pairs of objects to symbolize partnership and encourage love and harmonious relationships. The eastern-center area corresponds to the Family and Community of the Bagua Map, essential aspects of Pisceans. Introduce wood elements, like live plants, and water elements, like a water fountain, to promote a nurturing connection and environment within the family and community.

The center of the Bagua Map represents Health and Well-being. Blend earth-tone colours, representing the earth element, and a fireplace or a tall triangle-shaped decor piece, signifying the fire element, to build a tranquil and harmonious space with a focal point, such as a meditation area or a calming artwork, to support Pisces' need for inner peace.

Decorating with Feng Shui using the Bagua Map for the astrological sign Pisces is an artful way to align the home environment with the unique characteristics of this water sign. Incorporating water elements, promoting creativity, and fostering emotional connections create a space that resonates with Pisces' living environment, with the elemental energies complementing their astrological characteristics and personal and professional pursuits.

ASTROLOGY
INTERIOR DESIGN
CONSCIOUS LIFESTYLE

DISCOVER THE HIDDEN WORLD
OF ASTROLOGICAL DESIGN

REWARD

FRUITION ~ SUCCESS ~ FULFILLMENT

The mysterious marriage of Astrology and Interior Design can create an exceptionally supportive, personalized space that resonates with your individuality, your journey in life and the energies associated with your zodiac sign. Regardless of what the current designs are, successful Astrological Design enhances the quality of your life, productivity, and overall well-being while creating a personalized, visually and psychologically elevating space.

The unexplored world of Astrological Design offers an exotic, fascinating, mystical, and Avant-Garde approach to creating your living space, your temple that profoundly resonates with your personality and beliefs. You can experience a more auspicious or fortunate, more profound, healthier connection to yourself, your partner, family and environment, aligning with your instinctive gifts and aiding your natural progression in life.

Astrological Design takes a more holistic approach, forming spaces beyond current trends, aesthetics, and functionality. It encompasses psychological and spiritual aspects, promoting a well-rounded sense of comfort. It enhances self-discovery and encourages you to reflect on your personality, values, aspirations, and emotional needs.

REWARD

Interior Design and the age-old wisdom of Astrology urge you to make intentionally conscious choices, advancing you to a more aware, sensible, harmonious, and environmentally conscious way of living.

It can create an exclusive, chic space that challenges conventional norms or approaches, allowing for a more holistic and comprehensive creative expression that aligns with your astrological blueprint and ambiance.

Your home and personal space are an extension of you, directly echoing how you feel. Astrology can help you learn about your unique traits, empower you to align your living spaces with your natural gifts, dreams and desires, and allow you to set intentions for
inner transformation and personal growth.

By shaping your unique design style and personal space, and
aligning with your astrological traits and elements,
You tap into greater cosmic harmony,
creating environments that nurture your soul and
align with your spiritual essence, reflecting the
unique qualities of your zodiac blueprint.

REWARD

Blending your Astrological blueprint and heavenly nature into Interior Design extends your unique aura and flair to your home or office space, forming a spiritual dimension that resonates deeply with your natural being.

Just as celestial bodies influence your birth chart and life journey, and they also affect the energy and atmosphere within your spaces and personal surroundings.

Designing your private sanctuary, incorporating your Astrological Natal Chart, elevates your spaces beyond the physical. Your home is an exceptional environment to aid your ever-evolving self-development and personal transformation, which is spiritually enriching and aligns with your true nature.

This unconventional, mysterious, and uncharted path of astrological design will make you more holistic and environmentally friendly, improve your surroundings to support your life journey, personal growth and development, physical and mental health.
And enrich your emotional well-being.

www.ingramcontent.com/pod-product-compliance
Lightning Source LLC
Chambersburg PA
CBHW061157010526
44119CB00059B/847